PUZZLED PEOPLE

PUZZLED PEOPLE

A Study in Popular Attitudes to Religion, Ethics, Progress and Politics in a London Borough

PREPARED FOR THE ETHICAL UNION

by

MASS OBSERVATION

faber and faber

This edition first published in 2009
by Faber and Faber Ltd
Bloomsbury House, 74–77 Great Russell Street
London WC1B 3DA

Printed by CPI Antony Rowe, Eastbourne

All rights reserved
© Mass Observation, 1947

The right of the Mass Observation archive to be identified as author of this work
has been asserted in accordance with Section 77 of the
Copyright, Designs and Patents Act 1988

This book is sold subject to the condition that it shall not, by way of
trade or otherwise, be lent, resold, hired out or otherwise circulated
without the publisher's prior consent in any form of binding or cover other than
that in which it is published and without a similar condition including this
condition being imposed on the subsequent purchaser

A CIP record for this book is available from the British Library

ISBN 978–0–571–25148–3

CONTENTS

		PAGE
ETHICAL UNION'S PREFACE		7
I. PUZZLED PEOPLE		11
II. NEED FOR AN AIM?		14
III. THE GREAT MUDDLE		18
IV. BELIEF IN GOD		21
V. LIFE AFTER DEATH		27
VI. ORTHODOXY		42
VII. CHURCHGOING		50
VIII. PRAYER		53
IX. CHRIST'S TEACHING AND THE TEN COMMANDMENTS		62
X. WHAT IS RELIGION?		71
XI. ATTITUDES TO RELIGION		79
XII. TIME, RITUAL AND ETHICS		91
XIII. PURPOSE OF LIFE		98
XIV. THE MOST IMPORTANT THING		105
XV. ORGANISATION		119
XVI. PROGRESS AND SCIENCE		128
XVII. CLERGY'S VIEWS		139
SUMMARY OF CONCLUSIONS		156

MASS-OBSERVATION NOTES

1. Special attention is drawn to the more general material, outside religion, from p. 119 onwards. The results are summarised on p. 156 (see also p. 96).

2. In this report the sex, age and education of people whose comments are quoted is indicated by a simple code:

M = Male   F = Female.

Age assessed to the nearest five years.

El = Educated only up to the age of fourteen.

Sec = Educated after that age.

Thus, F45 El indicates a woman of about 45 with elementary education.

3. Mass-Observation has always held that it is part of its responsibility to endeavour to interpret the evidence it presents. In the present instance, particular care has been taken not to publish any interpretation which the material will not fully bear, since the subject is peculiarly one on which personal beliefs are liable to have a distorting effect. But this does not mean that alternative interpretations are necessarily invalid. Mr. Blackman, Secretary of the Ethical Union, who prefaces this book, leads the reader in suggesting implications which are, naturally, his own.

4. This particular Mass-Observation study was conducted throughout under the general control of H. D. Willcock.

5. Those interested may care to get hold of the following Mass-Observation surveys due for publication early in 1947:

Browns and Chester (Lindsay Drummond).

The Public and Foreign Affairs (Longmans).

Exmoor Village (Collins).

Social Research Methods (not yet in proof).

And a series of full-length surveys in the periodical *Contact*.

ETHICAL UNION'S PREFACE

THE SURVEY PRESENTED in the following report was undertaken by Mass-Observation at the instance of the Ethical Union, which financed the work of investigation. Our purpose was to study religious and kindred beliefs amongst a representative sample of ordinary people, and a typical urban area was selected for study. There is no pretence that this survey gives results which are definitely typical of the whole population; nor does it give an accurate measure of fundamental attitudes. But the nature of the comments made, and the figures so far as they go, give reliable general indications of the state of religious opinions and beliefs, and reveal prevalent tendencies.

None of those who will look with interest for the results of such an investigation will find any reason for satisfaction in these pages, unless he is prepared to be satisfied with the triumph of Roman Catholic indoctrination, or the ignorance and confusion of those who call themselves Christians, or the self-sufficient hedonism of crudely rationalist young men and the tendency of their views and ways to provide a model. The report reveals, at the level of opinion, a mental and moral chaos—the chaos of mass democracy.

The writer of the report suggests that the majority of people, on the findings of this investigation, are open to exploitation by any resolute opportunists with any ideology, because people are looking for something to believe; the explosion, or disintegration, of orthodox beliefs has left a vacuum which will be filled, and will be filled by worse if it is not soon filled by better. It is permissible to doubt that many of the people whose opinions were canvassed do want a view of the world in which they can believe, that they have found themselves bound to reject orthodox views and are looking for something in their place. No doubt there is in a great many minds little positive resistance to new ideologies, whatever they may be, but perhaps there is equally little receptivity. Possibly there are not many anywhere at any time who are of the stuff of which disciples are made. Perhaps the analogy of a vacuum, which is a figure of a temporary condition, should make us recall the Parable of the Sower, which is a figure of permanent characteristics of Nature. The vacuum is a local condition, created in this case by the decay of popular belief in orthodox Christianity. The winds of doctrine are always blowing, and sooner or later the vacuum will be filled. And the climate of opinion, under whose influence we all live, is created by the prevailing wind. But the Parable of the Sower reminds us that such vacuums occur as more or less isolated air-pockets. That is to say, the hard core of the problem is in those many who are permanently indifferent to any doctrine, not in the few who have lost their beliefs. There are here two problems, closely related, but not the same, and to confuse them will lead to radical errors of diagnosis and prescription.

It is impossible to escape a pessimistic conclusion if we look at the problem from the point of view of an ideology, whatever it may be. If we are trying to make orthodox Christians, or Marxists or independent rationalists in the liberal tradition, then we must think only of a small minority and not of the masses. But the problem is a problem of the masses. It is fair to suggest that this report tends to confirm the view that an ideological approach to this problem is inappropriate and obsolescent. The correct modern approach is sociological, for it is more than belief which has suffered disintegration. The leaders of thought, and their followers, should be thinking far less of converting the masses to their views than of influencing their practice (their behaviour, their habits, their interests) by influencing their situation, by taking part themselves in the creation of new forms and opportunities of social and personal life. The principles of Christianity and the principles of liberal rationalism have failed to save the masses from desultory living. Any other ideology will succeed no better. It remains for us to see what transforming the conditions of life and thought will do, by wise and large application of the principles of the Peckham Health Centre, of the Community Centres and Village Colleges, of Town and Country Planning, of the new Education Act. Such means as these, properly understood and developed, promise a transformation of the individual by a new social integration which no party means can effect on a mass scale—unless the party has unlimited power. This is a hard lesson for the leaders of thought and their followers. But it is one which should be learned, because it is they who can do most to develop and fulfil the finest uses of these new social methods and instruments. It is a lesson which this report may help to enforce. If so, the report not only indicates, at the level of opinion, the deplorable condition of the people, but will also make a contribution to the new social practice by which we may all hope to attain in common at least the early stages of regeneration. For this lesson, as the evidence in the last chapter of the report brings out, applies no less to the political leaders and their followers than to the leaders of thought and theirs: the creation of faith in democracy is not less urgent than the creation of faith in purposive living. Apart from the new social techniques, the moral is an old one, a permanent truth—namely, that religious and political leadership, local and national, belongs properly to those who seek and renew it by full personal participation in the life and opportunities of the people. Creative democracy is genuinely that, and nothing else. Prophetic religion was that. If it is a counsel of perfection in our complicated bureaucratic society, it is not therefore to be disregarded but rather to be vehemently proclaimed. The social planning which is our destiny makes its practice more imperative and more possible.

I record, with personal appreciation, our gratitude to the staff of Mass-Observation, who from first to last made the inquiry their own, and conducted the investigation with a keen public spirit.

H. J. BLACKHAM,
General Secretary, the Ethical Union.

42 CHANDOS HOUSE,
BUCKINGHAM GATE, S.W.1.

I

PUZZLED PEOPLE

1. "There must be something with all these terrible things happening. It couldn't be just Fate or natural causes. It must be something got the power to do it. We was going down and all of a sudden we've come up. I've seen on the pictures people who can't talk or do anything, like in these Tarzan films, they say we was come from monkeys. There must be some human being above us, to give us all these ideas and that" (F35 El).

2. "Well, I don't know; you get on the best way you can. I've had my share of trouble and by what I can see the Almighty don't listen to you when you pray, so what's the use? Sometimes I think there must be something in it, but most times I think there's nothing to it at all. Religion and all that sort of thing, I mean" (F45 El).

3. "I didn't come of a religious family and my husband's not religious and I don't think a lot of religious people; it's something I never bother with. Of course, I think you should do right as much as you can, I don't mean people should live, anyhow. But I don't see that going to church and doing a lot of praying in public and putting your money in the collection plate is going to do much good. I think people don't believe in that sort of thing any more. It was the fashion once. It isn't nowadays" (F19 El).

4. "I never took no interest in it, not after I stopped going to Sunday school. I think you can get along very well in life without worrying about things like that—it's only a worry after all. I think you can see for yourself if a thing's right or wrong, you don't need to waste your Sunday going listening to parsons. After all, they're only in it for the money—it's their living, like another man's—I don't think they really teach you anything you couldn't know of yourself, if you've got any sense" (M25 El).

5. "There's a lot of good people in the world, but the people that call themselves Christians are the sort that go to church and put 'No Hawkers. No Circulars. Keep Out' on their gate and wouldn't do a kindness to anybody under the sun. And that's why I'm not in favour of Christianity" (M35 El).

6. "I think it'll be like H. G. Wells says in his books. There'll be bigger and bigger wars, because they're doing terrible things now, and there's bound to be another war. Of course, it'll take thousands and thousands of years, but in the end mankind will destroy itself. I suppose it is progress in a way" (F25 El).

7. "Progressing? I don't call it progressing. I calls it progressing the wrong way. Making all of us into machines. What I would call progress would be to make everything beautiful for people to live in and helping poor people who really need it and things like that. I call that progress. But my son always says there's going to be a revolution in this country. He says: 'There's never been a revolution in this country, but there's going to be. Things have been too much the one way round' " (F60 El).

And so on. This book is an attempt to show the puzzledness of ordinary people about some of the main stabilities of the past, especially religion. The basic framework is a random sample cross-section of 500 interviews with the inhabitants of a London semi-suburban borough, Metrop, supplemented by informal conversations with others on various topics under discussion, by investigations among Mass-Observation's National Panel of Observers (who answer written questions by post), by talks with Metrop clergymen and youth leaders, and by a consideration of voluminous related material already on our files. It is not a technical book and we have tried to present the facts as simply and clearly as possible without excessive methodological discussion.

There is no pretence that the numerical results of the survey are "typical" of the country as a whole. They are not. On the other hand, they probably differ little from those which would be obtained in any suburban area of a big city to-day. A village would typically show different results (in this connection see forthcoming Adprint book *Exmoor Village*, based on an M.-O. rural survey). But while the figures here are precisely representative of nothing but Metrop, the types of attitude we describe *are* typical of the attitude of millions of people all over the country to-day. It is a matter of purely academic interest to determine within the nearest 10 or 100,000 precisely how many people in Britain hold these views. Such exact quanta can only at present be measured at the top level of verbal interview. Here, as in all points of questioning, including those that follow in this book, it must be appreciated that the percentage "opinion" of to-day changes to-morrow and may be totally reversed next year. It is the *underlying* causes, motives and drives which the sociologist must delve for, and which alone have some sort of permanent validity, the quality remaining through all quantitative change.

II

NEED FOR AN AIM?

It is a commonplace of human behaviour that like-minded people tend to group themselves together. If this were not so, if friends and companions were chosen by the shape of their ears or the length of their toes, there would be little need for a report of the kind we present here. The sort of facts which sociology, opinion research, social research, collects and presents are intrinsically the most "obvious" facts of all. They make interesting reading, and sometimes lead to useful action, largely because people don't bother much about others with whom they have little in common. The area of personal acquaintanceship is usually confined mainly to birds of a feather, and we most of us have only the haziest idea of the thoughts, words and actions of the great outer circle—ninety-nine point something per cent. of the people in the next few streets.

The exception is, or should be, the specialist whose job it is to bring others to his way of thinking. A conscientious parish priest or an active worker in the atheist movement should, if he knows his job, get little more than a confirmation of his own observations from this report. But both are skilled occupations, and the possession of strong views of one's own does not help in assessing the ideas of others. Unless people hold their opinions very strongly, they usually water them down to suit the ears of the known partisan. So priest and atheist may both be surprised at times.

The general gist of the first part of this report is that most people nowadays don't think much about religion, don't set much conscious store by it, and have decidedly confused ideas about it. Many of those whose outlook might be described thus will be reading these words. They may well say: "So what? I don't care much. Others don't care much. Who cares? Why write a book about it?"

The answer in the present case is not simply that part of Mass-Observation's and sociology's job is to record the present. M.-O. is not professionally concerned with the rights and wrongs of the long-held beliefs which are becoming so widely rejected to-day; that is a something for the individual to assess for himself. We do consider it part of our responsibility, however, to attempt an interpretation of the evidence at our disposal. If long-standing ideas have been wrong, it may be good that people reject them; if things which have taken an important place in people's lives at other periods are of little moment, it may be good that people should not waste time over them. But if nothing succeeds these beliefs, then there is a vacuum, and what hot air comes rushing in to take their place is very much a matter of what hot air there is about.

There have been many periods of scepticism and cynicism in history. It is doubtful whether there has ever before been a time when scepticism and cynicism have been such easy subjects for exploitation by equally cynical leadership—or by the cynic *manqué* turned prophet. Moreover, the state of mind of many people to-day is somewhat hastily and inadequately characterised as cynical or sceptical. A "healthy scepticism" is something which we can all recognise as a positive state, though some would welcome and others deplore its existence. The sceptic is on the alert, though he may be as gullible as anyone else if the right note is struck. He has a creed. But the situation to-day is a much more negative one. People are losing interest in many of the things which used to be accepted fairly widely and fairly deeply. A sort of inert agnosticism exists on many subjects, without any corresponding vitality attached to the superseding belief—indeed, often without any corresponding belief at all.

People, it seems, do need some norm against which to measure themselves. If, in the inter-war words of Cole Porter, "Anything goes," society is not yet in a sufficiently paradisical state for each of its members to work out his or her own destiny from scratch. People still need standards and some sort of prescribed common aim as a yardstick; otherwise they become confused and are more liable to have no beliefs than to work out their own. Of such nihilistic material spurious and cynical doctrines can, and do, make their vanguard and most ardent agents. While it is doubtless better that people should be taught *how* to think rather than what to think, if they are not taught the former they cannot by themselves learn the latter. It is as much good crying, "Opinion is free. You can think what you like," to people who do not know how to form an opinion as it is to present a library to a man who has not been taught to read. Freedom of opinion is the life blood of democracy, but (as with any other freedom) people are at sea unless they know how to use it. The implicit overall moral of this report is that very many *are* to-day lost in this wilderness of free opinion; that they *want* extraneous standards and are at sea without them. Life, deprived of many of the ready-made aims and targets which it held for our grandparents, calls for much more original thought from ordinary people, and there are signs that many of them are standing up badly to the strain.

Diversity of positive opinion and belief is a healthy sign. Uninformed, misinformed, underinformed and inconsistent opinions and beliefs are not. Nor is it necessarily, *ipso facto*, a healthy sign if opinion questions previously accepted beliefs and dogmas. We have to see with what new ideas the blank spaces are being filled. If there are no new ideas, then something is being lost for which a more up-to-date substitute has not yet been found; the imperfect is being destroyed simply because it seems imperfect, and not because a more perfect replacements exists. If the same thing happened with commodities, the public, deprived of the accustomed article, might well rush to buy an inferior one of a new make. It can happen with ideas. Sustained scepticism and cynicism over a wide area of opinion and belief is a hard exercise in intellectual discipline: and intellectual stamina is as much dependent on training as physical endurance. The great majority of people have not had the requisite training. They cannot reject indefinitely without accepting, and the more completely they reject one thing the greater is their need likely to become to accept another in its place. There is no guarantee that the substitute will be superior; indeed, the more urgent the need, the more likelihood of an *ersatz* product filling the gap.

Whatever the personal views of the reader may be, it would be rash for him to assume that, because some of the disbeliefs and scepticisms which this report documents correspond with his own, *therefore* all is well. All is not well because people are right about what's wrong. They can still go wrong about what's right—indeed, the longed-for *ersatz* right may well be wronger than the rejected wrong. Events in the past two decades have shown what crazy, sinister, and elaborate structures can be built in minds empty of firm aims and ideals. If enough is rejected long enough and not replaced, the critical faculties may be impaired. To have rejected the imperfect does not exclude the possibility of accepting the inane later. It may even be a desirable condition precedent. A thoroughly woolly ethic may be better protection against still woollier ethics than no ethic at all. Someone is going to cash in on these wide open spaces in the mind; we must be careful that it is not some speculating jerry-builder of illusion. Otherwise the mental slums of Britain in 1965 may present the same vast problems as those of Germany to-day.

If this report is a depressing one for the priest and the idealist, it also contains an implicit warning to the atheist and agnostic. Of such was the kingdom of Hitler.

III

THE GREAT MUDDLE

OF THE DOUBTERS, AGNOSTICS and atheists in Metrop, over a quarter say they pray on occasions to the God whose existence they doubt. One in twelve went to church within the past six months, compared with one in three of those who say they believe in God. Over half the non-believers consider that there should be religious education in schools.

Of those who say they believe in a Deity, one in five are definite in their assertion that they do not believe in a life after death; one-half say they never go to church, or only go for weddings, funerals and such-like. A quarter never pray or pray only in church.

Of those who attend Church of England services regularly or intermittently, one-quarter do not believe in an after-life; on the other hand, one-fifth of those who don't go to church at all do believe. Of those who don't believe in a Deity or are agnostic, nearly a quarter tend to think that Christ was "something more than a man"; on the other hand, a rather larger proportion of Church of England churchgoers say he was *only* a man. Of those who say he was only a man, one in five also say they believe he was born of a virgin. But of those who attend Church of England services, one in four doubt the doctrine of the Virgin Birth and only one in three give quite definite assent to it.

This is a brief preview of some of the confusions of thought and attitude which exist to-day on the subject of religion. Taken in isolation, some of the points which we shall discuss here may seem encouraging to the religious, some to the atheist. Interrelated, there is little which can cause much elation to either or, for that matter, to anyone between the extremes, whose views hold a degree of consistency. For this reason, we jump into the middle of the subject at the outset. We have had a good deal of experience of the frequency with which well-meaning partisans tear facts from their context when they wish to illustrate their point; and in the present instance we feel that such use of the material would be particularly unfortunate.

It is of the essence of a Mass-Observation report that it attempts a thorough objective diagnosis before suggesting a cure. This report is a diagnosis of a social malady whose ultimate consequence may be disastrous if its course is not checked. To pick out a symptom and concentrate on its eradication without reference to related symptoms may be worse than useless. Those who read this book with an eye to the furtherance of their particular ideological cause will find no lack of ammunition; but they should bear in mind the fact that, essentially, we are demonstrating the existence of a vacuum in several compartments of peoples' minds. To fill compartment A with doctrines of the cause will not get far if compartment B is to be filled with those of another cause. In fact, very much this process has resulted in the present bewilderment and apathy. Ordinary people have never before been presented with so many ideas as in the past century or so; there have never been so many people equipped, in an elementary way, to deal with ideas. Yet the result is not that people are bubbling over with ideas, but rather that they have fewer of a positive kind than they had when the field was more limited and their comprehension was restricted by lack of training.

The problem presented is not simply: "Here is an empty space. What shall we build in it?" It is· "Here are a series of vacant sites, undermined with an explosive charge which has, already, destroyed buildings that have stood there for generations. The explosive, compounded of liberal education and free access to the logic of events, is of our own making and we do not wish to remove it. What structure will be strong enough to withstand its blast?"

In other words, a temporary makeshift solution may well be much worse than no solution at all. As reason explodes beneath the elaborate superstructure which National Socialism built up in people's minds, scattered mental bric-à-brac may take longer to clear than the physical destruction of war.

If there is danger of the people of this country reaching that profoundly negative state of mind which made Nazism possible in 1933, then, very likely, it will be only *too* easy to fill the spaces with illusion or reality. And it may well be a profitable short-term investment for the merchants of illusion.

With these few words of "warning," we may proceed to discuss the material in natural sequence.

IV

BELIEF IN GOD

METROP PEOPLE WERE ASKED: "Do you believe there is a God, or there isn't, or haven't you made up your mind?"

About two-thirds of men and four-fifths of women said they did believe, or believed more or less. One man in three and one woman in five expressed definite doubt, mostly saying that their mind was not made up. Altogether, one in twenty of Metrop citizens are uncompromising disbelievers in a deity, and these are mostly men.

In all that follows, we call "believers" those who believe more or less, and "non-believers" those who disbelieve more or less.

The grouping of the small minority of expressed atheists with the larger group of doubters is somewhat arbitrary—actually more so than appears at first sight—but in considering related attitudes which tend to fall naturally into parallel groups it will be found adequate.

General Trends and Group Differences

The difference between the sexes, with women more inclined to unqualified faith in God, is one which runs through all religious attitudes, and from casual observation, will cause no one much surprise. It is worth noticing, however, that this female "acceptance" is by no means confined to questions of faith. It is a very general pattern of women's attitude as compared with men's, on all subjects. Women are regularly more inclined to accept, or welcome, the *fait accompli* than men, and less inclined to criticise the *status quo*. Thus new legislation frequently finds more acceptance among women than men, though women often lag behind men in finding fault with established ideas and procedure. In accepting God, woman is behaving according to the frequent thought processes of her sex.

In all, one person in four openly doubts the existence of a Deity, one in twenty expressing definitely atheistic views. There are exactly twice as many non-believers among the younger generation as among the old—36 per cent. of the under-forties and 18 per cent. of the over-forties. This ratio of 2 to 1 non-believers between old and young is consistent with other surveys made by Mass-Observation on wider samples and using various methods to reveal various facets of attitude; and a similar ratio holds between men and women. In all questions relating to religion we have to consider very carefully the extent to which people are liable to answer as they feel they should, rather than giving their true views. Attention is drawn in later discussion to "prestige" answers, but in the present instance the indications are that social compulsions play a relatively small part.[1] Most of the non-believers would probably stick to their views in argument.

There was no difference at all between the attitude of more and less educated people on this point. Virtually identical proportions of those with secondary and with elementary education fall into the two main groups of believers and non-believers.

Belief and War

"Yes, I think there is a God, but He seems a bit preoccupied at the moment," said a twenty-year-old girl. "I don't really know," said a middle-aged working man. "I don't suppose anybody really knows, with all these wars going on. He ought to do something about it."

There were numerous remarks instancing war and the state of the world as a reason for doubting the existence of a Deity. Examples:

[1] Other questions asked at various times have included, "What are your own religious beliefs?" and "Are you religious or not?" The former question, because of the implication that *some* belief is expected produces a slightly lower proportion of non-believers than the present one. But the difference is very slight, indicating that most people falling into this group have fairly firm views. The latter question produces a *much* higher proportion of apparent non-believers than the present one, because of the social implications of the phrase "being religious," which ties up with church-going and over-piousness. In this study we are aiming at depth and not at precise statistics, but the general indications from a variety of sources are that religion plays practically no part in the lives of between one in four and one in five people, at a conscious level at least.

"I haven't made up my mind, but when I look round I don't think there can be" (F35 Sec).

"It's hard to reconcile the fact of God with this terrible thing. If this is divine justice, it's a bit hard, I think" (M30 Sec).

"I'm not sure that there is a God. If there is one, why should He allow all the terrible things that are happening. I think He could have prevented a lot of this massacre" (F34 El).

"I don't know, and I'll tell you for why. If there's a God about you'd think He wouldn't allow all these awful things to happen, and step in and stop them" (F25 El).

Taken in isolation, frequent comments of this sort might suggest that the experience of war has turned people away from belief in God. Previous Mass-Observation surveys, however, indicate that those who make this type of remark are mostly those who had no very definite faith before. Four studies were made in 1941-2 to assess the effects of war on religious belief and attitude. The general conclusions reached were as follows: War has produced a trend away from religion among those with no pronounced beliefs before. The proportion who feel they have *lost* their faith, however, is very small—between 1-4 per cent. in all the samples studied. The indications are that major disillusionment with religion because of the war is confined almost entirely to those who never paid much more than lip-service to it before. In general the wartime trend is for those with a fairly deep faith to have had their beliefs strengthened; and for those whose faith played little part in their lives before to have had it weakened still further.

In other words, war has cleared the air to some extent, but it has not greatly disturbed the general distribution of faith and lack of faith. It has for the most part confirmed and strengthened pre-existing attitudes rather than changed them.

Agnosticism

By an agnostic is usually meant a person who believes that it is impossible to know, rather than someone who is merely undecided. On this definition there are very few agnostics in Metrop. One of the most frequent replies among those who did not feel able to commit themselves either way, was to say that they sometimes thought one thing, sometimes another. Some of the younger generation:

"Well, half and half. Sometimes I think there is one and sometimes I don't! Not when I see good people suffer and the bad getting on" (M24 El).

"At times I believe in it and at times I don't. I neither believe nor disbelieve" (M35 El).

"Well, I suppose there may be. You have to take it in trust. And there's times you don't feel inclined to" (M22 El).

"Well, sometimes I do and sometimes I don't. It's all according" (F35 El).

"Sometimes I do think there must be somebody, and then I have my doubts" (F35 El).

A distinction should be made between this type of attitude and agnosticism. Most of these people do not believe that the existence of God is unknowable: they simply vacillate between belief and disbelief according to circumstance, which is a very different and less satisfactory matter.

Atheists

Definite disbelief was expressed by one person in twenty, predominantly by young men. There was a note of protest in many of the replies, which probably means that these young people are little more secure in their disbelief than the doubters in their doubt:

"No, not on your life" (M30 El).

"No. I don't. That's all a tale. People used to think they had to believe it, but now they think different" (M27 El).

"No, it's all a lot of hooey" (F31 El).

In between fall the more positive doubters, the comparatively few who show signs of making some sort of a struggle to reach a decision; and those, fewer still, who have come to the conclusion that they can't know. For the most part the disbelievers' attitudes are essentially negative; they not only don't know, but they don't care. In this respect many of the believers' attitudes are very similar. The thirty-year-old man who said, "Yes, there's a God all right, but I don't bother with these things," is prototype of many others, who are inevitably classified numerically with the believers. While, in this part of the investigation, we did not attempt to get below the surface of stranger-interview, it was clear enough that some people were digging up rusty ideas from the past in order to give a reply at all, and were repeating formula rather than making a statement about a subject of importance in their lives. These lessons learnt long ago and resuscitated for the occasion sometimes looked suspect even to those who had learnt them:

"Oh yes, I believe there is. But whether I've just been brought up to believe it as a child I don't know" (F30 El).

"Well, I've always been brought up to believe, but you do wonder, sometimes. I don't think I can argue on it" (F30 El).

"I couldn't say, we're only told there is one, and I suppose we must believe in one" (M17 El).

"Well, I have my doubts now, but in our religion we have to believe in a God. You either do or you don't. I have my doubts, but my wife hasn't. Perhaps it's because I read too much" (M40 El).

Whichever side of the fence these superficial verbal comments may fall, the underlying attitude is clearly not a stable one. The number of people who have any *stable* belief in the existence of a Deity is much smaller than the number who merely give assent. One of the most revealing comments of all came from the man who said:

"Now you're asking me an unfair question. I don't believe there is such a thing, but it's a good thing to have it instilled into people so that there's something if the man needs it" (M39 El).

Possibly there is no God, but it doesn't do to be too sure, otherwise what is there to turn to in trouble? How many people to-day stay on the sunny side of disbelief for something approaching this reason? More important, how many are in that receptive state where they will only too readily embrace any more tangible earthly substitute for so questionable a heavenly comforter? Part of the answer can be found by examining the implications of those somewhat diffuse attitudes which we have characterised as "belief" and "disbelief" in God.

V

LIFE AFTER DEATH

IT HAS LONG BEEN one of the main planks in the militant atheists' platform that belief in God induces people to accept the injustices of life too passively. If we relate belief in a Deity to belief in life after death, we find that those who doubt the existence of a Deity are fairly consistent in doubting the possibility of a hereafter. *But,* two out of five of those who say they believe in God are by no means sure that there is any life after death, half of these being fairly convinced that there isn't.

Though no organised system of belief in this country which postulates the existence of a Deity does not also postulate life after death in some form, personal beliefs to-day are often remote from the tenets of organised religion. The above gives a preliminary indication of the extent of this deviation from established creeds.

They may also suggest, to those who find difficulty in understanding the conception of a Deity solely devoted to the affairs of this earth, that there is muddle somewhere; but they do not prove it. A more relevant figure is the distribution of beliefs among those who attend Church services.

Correlating attitudes to life after death with churchgoing, we find:

Attitude to Life after Death	Don't go to Church:	Go to Church of England Churches:
Believe, or incline to believe (including re-incarnation)	32	54
Disbelieve, incline to disbelieve, undecided	68	46

Percentage having this attitude among those who—

As one Church of England priest in Metrop commented:

"I don't know what people believe when they say the Creed. I've been attending a death in a religious house, and mentioned life after death. And they say, 'Is there really any life after death? I didn't know there was any.'"

Group Differences

The difference between men and women's attitudes is the usual one, with women much more inclined to believe than men, as they are to believe in a Deity. But nearly half the women, and nearly two-thirds of the men, incline to think there is no afterlife, or are undecided about it. The difference between young and old, however, is comparatively small—under 1 in 10—though there are many more non-believers among younger people.

On the other hand, though there is no significant difference among more and less educated people so far as expressed belief in God is concerned, there is a major difference in their attitude to life after death:

> 66 per cent. of those with *secondary* education say they believe in life after death.
>
> 41 per cent. of those with *elementary* education say this.

At first sight, this seems to run counter to the general pattern of greater scepticism among the more educated which we find on more specific questions of faith. An examination of the verbatim comments, however, shows that the less educated are often rejecting a different thing from the more educated when they say they do not believe in an afterlife. This trend is shown partly in the comments of the believers, and partly in those of the non-believers. Several of the less educated believers thought it necessary to say that the afterlife they believed in was *not* the old-fashioned Heaven and Hell, or that they did not believe people lived on in their earthly bodies. On the other hand, some of the less educated disbelievers were clearly rejecting a similar conception, like the old man of seventy-five who said:

> "I don't believe I shall ever have wings. There aren't any men angels. I've never seen any pictures of them, only women angels and baby angels" (M75 El).

Or this sixty-year-old's comment:

> "I believe when you're dead, you're dead. I've never seen any angels. I don't want to" (M60 El).

These are extremes, but it is clear that many of the less educated do not mean the same thing as the more educated by life after death, and that their conception is easier to reject and more difficult to accept. While the less educated are rejecting hell fire and harps, and often have no other idea to put in their place, the conception of the more educated does *not* include these things. This does not alter the fact that the educated are more inclined to believe in an afterlife, but it does show that their belief is mainly due to their having a different and subtler conception rather than a lesser degree of scepticism.

Reincarnation

The conception of life after death was explored at various levels—by long informal conversations and through the written comments of Mass-Observation's National Panel. Perhaps the least expected, and in some ways the most significant, fact which came to light was the extent of belief in reincarnation. Among the interview sample about one person in twenty-five *spontaneously* went into enough detail to show that they held some such belief. That amounts to about one in ten of those who have any definite belief in an afterlife at all, and is almost certainly an underestimate, since no attempt was made by direct questioning to go into the details of people's conception.

Another index is given by a question on their attitudes to death and dying, asked of the National Panel. It is reasonable to suppose that, in a detailed written discussion of this sort, those who set much store by their conceptions of what comes after would mention them in connection with their attitude to death. In fact, two-thirds mentioned an afterlife, and of these rather less than half tended to believe in it, the rest being undecided or disbelieving.

This National Panel is a special group of more than average intelligence and thoughtfulness, but the results show much the same pattern as the less specialised investigation— about one person in three not really interested in the subject either way, and the rest consisting of rather more agnostics and disbelievers than believers. The chief difference was that among the "intelligent" people there were more agnostics and fewer disbelievers. But, as we have already shown, the greater disbelief of the less educated can largely be put down to the fact that many of them have nothing to put in the place of hell fire and harps; we should expect more agnosticism at a higher educational level, where complete rejection is a less simple matter.

Among the more "intelligent" sample there was a rather more frequent belief in reincarnation than among the broader group.

The significance of this belief—not included in the dogmas of any religious system at all widely adhered to in this country—would appear to lie in its materialistic character. The conception of a spiritual or non-corporeal existence is not required, and the mind used to seeing everything in material terms finds less to boggle at.

To say this is in no way to evaluate the belief, but it does provide one possible explanation of its widespread acceptance to-day. If we examine the verbatim comments, we shall see that they range down to concepts which do not require any faith in the supernatural at all. On the borderline of belief in reincarnation are those who believe that we live on in our children. The simplest specific expression of belief in reincarnation, however, is one remove from this. In the words of a woman of fifty-five:

"I think that we come up again as somebody else. Like another person—another branch of the family. There are often two people that resemble one another. You can see them; they've got all the same ways and there's such a strong resemblance" (F53 El).

An example of the simpler "rational" basis for believing in reincarnation comes from this old man:

"Well, according to books and reading, they say you return in a different form. I would say there's life in you after you're dead. Did you know your hair grows after you're buried? So that proves there is" (M70 El).

One or two people expressed a belief in the transmigration of souls:

"I don't think there's a Heaven or a future life for the spirit or anything like that. We all come back as other forms of life—a caterpillar or a worm or something. Or even a vegetable, meself, I think" (M60 El).

But this was very infrequent. The usual attitude was that the dead return to earth again as people, and it varied from the simpler conceptions outlined to the more complex (and more orthodox), belief in a series of lives each on a higher plane. Two examples from the written comments of middle-class women:

"I believe in a series of human lives, and when one has learnt what one has to learn from them, I think the spiritual life goes on in conditions which I am unable to imagine. Death will be a new adventure—interesting. Perhaps one is much more free. Does the butterfly remember the chrysalis, let alone the larva? Time shackles us now—perhaps we shall not be bounded by it then. Of course, we shall in other human lives, but not for ever."

"My general feelings about death now are that anyone dead has got all out of this life he/she was sent here to experience, and has, so to speak, gone to another room awaiting a further excursion into this world. Very surprised that I feel like this, as I used to consider myself too intelligent for fairy-tale religion."

Among those who say they believe in an afterlife, there are many whose beliefs can scarcely be called religious in any accepted sense. They believe in continuity, and have given the name life-after-death to commonplace experiences:

"I think when you're dead, it's the spirit of the good you've done on earth that lives on. If you've done kind actions, that's your afterlife. My dad used to say: 'You say my Dad did that.' It's your memory" (F50 El).

"I'm afraid I haven't figured it out. I've thought about it, but I'm dubious. I do believe we shall. . . . Each human being has a place in the universe, and life after death is the things they've done . . . ashes to ashes, you know . . . (M30 Sec).

This attitude, and the above-mentioned belief that people "live on" in their children, seem fairly close to the belief that people are reincarnated either into the family or with some memories of past existence. As one middle-class housewife wrote:

> "I definitely really believe that I shall be reborn in another incarnation, and that I shall remember a little of now, and be very interested in new developments."

Heaven

Whether the reader looks upon belief in an afterlife as a matter of spiritual faith or intellectual credulity, it is clear that less exertion of the faculty is needed for this range of attitude than for the more orthodox beliefs of Christian doctrines. In some cases, indeed, it seems that "life after death" is little more than a remembered phrase tagged on to a commonplace earthly experience. Belief in a Deity not only does not necessarily imply belief in life after death, but where it does the afterlife is often as remote from the "pie in the sky" Heaven of atheist satire as it is from the concepts of the Christian Churches. Nevertheless, the idea of an afterlife which will "make up," in a very material sense, for the defects of earthly existence is not infrequent. An Anglo-Catholic Vicar in Metrop generalised about his own experiences with his parishioners:

> "They talk glibly about Heaven and the angels, and think their children are going to be little angels in a place where some of the frightful difficulties now besetting them just *are not*. Like Oliver Lodge and Raymond . . . who was supposed to have said there was very good whisky there. They hope there'll be very good beer."

A believer in reincarnation writes:

> "As I have continuous evil health, head and tummy and liver trouble eternally, the next incarnation, I expect, will be in a world where I shall get treatment from birth, and I shall enjoy life a lot more."

And two working-class women said:

"Oh well, I've got great faith in a better existence after this one, and so has my husband. But I'm sure I don't know what you do with your time. I don't think you can waste it in enjoying yourself, I sort of think you have a nice long rest and then find something to do."

"Well, I dunno. You think different things at different times. You're never taught anything about that—you have to imagine it for yourself. I do think if there's anything, it'll be better than this. It couldn't be a lot worse, could it? And I think you'll see the people you love again, or there wouldn't be any point in it. What always puzzled me was, people that believe anything never seem to think there'll be any work there. People will just sit around enjoying themselves. I don't know about that, myself. I've always worked. I wouldn't know what to do with myself."

The compensatory Heaven, a better life rather in the physical sense implied by a higher standard of living than in any ethical or spiritual sense, is certainly a fairly frequent conception. Harps and wings are being discarded from the picture, and many have not arrived at an alternative expectation. But many of those who have still visualise Heaven in an equally material way—either as a return to earth, or as life in another world made only the more mundane by the elimination of angels.

Priests and parsons with whom the attitude of their parishioners was discussed mostly agreed in saying that those who believed in an afterlife did so in a very vague way:

"Yes. Goodness knows what sort. Sometimes at a funeral one of them will say to me, 'Well, it's a happy release,' and I say to them, 'I wonder.' They most of them look forward after death to some hope of conditions that are easier—an escape from the troubles of life. And certainly there are a few spiritualistic ideas floating about in their heads" (Church of England Vicar).

And it was not always clear that the parson did not to some extent share the bewilderment of his parishioners:

"It's hard to say—some do and some don't; some seem mainly content to leave it. There's a lot of vague spiritualistic ideas. They say, 'You can't *know*,' and I agree with them. They've repudiated the old-fashioned ideas of Heaven and Hell. I've recommended them to see *Between Two Worlds*, showing that Heaven and Hell can be the same place" (Methodist).

"I think the majority of people find it difficult to think of themselves not existing, if I may put it that way. But in any case it's all very vague—even the teaching of the churches on that point is not very definite. Nothing much outside the Book of Revelation, and all sorts of cranks have all sorts of explanations about that. It's had an interest for many quite intelligent people, but they all have different theories about it—it does attract people with a kink in their minds. The general teaching of the Christian faith is to concentrate on the present life and leave the future in the hands of God. The spiritualist mediums have had an influence, but that's vague again. People pick one thing that seems to apply to them personally, and that makes them credulous about the rest" (Church of England).

Rejection

One person in three says without qualification that he or she does not believe in life after death, and for the most part these rejections seem fairly clear-cut and definite:

"No! We come up and bloom for the age; that's all" (M50 El).
"Death ends everything. You're finished when you die; that's my opinion" (M19 El).
"Once we're dead, we're dead" (M 35 El).
"Death is the end. I don't think there's anything to come after" (F30 El).

Of the rest, about half are fairly definite in saying that they believe in an afterlife, and the other half in various stages of indecision. Disbelief and indecision is only a little less frequent among those who attend Church of England services than it is among people as a whole. A fifth of those who say they believe in God, and a quarter of those who go to Church of England services, are definite in their disbelief in life after death; another fifth of each are undecided.

Does it Matter?

It can hardly be disputed that these facts indicate some confusion. But confusion of attitude and inconsistency between attitudes is not an unusual thing when people are *not particularly interested* in a subject. In itself, the confusion outlined will point different ways to different people, according to their own beliefs; to some it may simply suggest that many do not trouble to think much about the subject; to others it may suggest inadequate teaching on the part of the Church; to others it may indicate that the rationalist viewpoint has at least made some headway among the general population, that the ground is being cleared.

On their own, in fact, these results are so ambiguous that any interpretation is highly speculative. We need some better indication of the importance of these things in people's lives. If they are passing over the idea of life after death as something which doesn't concern them much either way, then the conclusion to be drawn is different from what it might be if they were deeply concerned and unable to arrive at a definite conclusion. This is a point which cannot be reliably tackled in a direct way, since people are unlikely to be fully aware themselves of the underlying importance of their attitudes, much less to discuss them at these deeper levels.

One clue is the current popularity of spiritualism; and, perhaps, at another level, the vacillations of belief in astrology. These we discuss later in conjunction with prayer, when much of the foregoing materials is re-presented in the light of further evidence. Important indirect evidence is afforded, however, from quite another source.

The Popular Fade-out

In April, 1940, the *Sunday Dispatch* set a competition awarding prizes for what readers considered the best film fade-out they had seen. By courtesy of the film critic, the entries, 577 in number, were handed to Mass-Observation, and a detailed analysis was made of them. Each entrant named three fade-outs, and in all 354 different films were mentioned.

The most popular fade-outs were as follows:

First. Three Comrades. Here two of the comrades, already dead, beckon the third to join them. Arm in arm, the three comrades march through the skies.

Second. Dark Victory. The heroine walks slowly upstairs to die, bravely and alone.

Third. Good-bye, Mr. Chips. Mr. Chips in his old age murmurs as he dies the names of the boys he has known.

Fourth. Wuthering Heights. The hero climbs the hill, faithful to a tryst with a lover who is dead.

Fifth. A Tale of Two Cities. Carton says: "It is a far, far better thing," etc. The camera pans as the guillotine knife falls, and shows the clear sky. Then a Scripture text.

Sixth. Modern Times. Charlie Chaplin and the girl walk off down the road together.

Seventh. Queen Christina. The exiled Queen stands at the prow of the ship, like a figurehead, looking into the future.

Eighth. Lost Horizon. The hero struggles back over the mountains to the dream city of Shangri La.

Before commenting on this, let us consider the following analysis of the total entry. Fade-outs were grouped under thirteen heads, according to the actual visual content of the ending. Most of the categories are self-explanatory, but the following need a word of explanation:

Death: Fade-outs on dead bodies.
Bereavement: Fade-outs on those suffering loss of friends, etc.
Supernatural: Fade-outs with the spirits of the dead.
Hope: Fade-outs with characters looking forward to a better future.
Self-denial: Fade-outs on lovers parting, mother leaving children, etc.

The percentages referring to each type of ending showed a most striking similarity between men and women, there being a difference of only 1 per cent. between the sexes in over half the cases, and a maximum difference of 5 per cent.

Results were:

Content of Fade-out	Percentage mentioning Fade-out with this Content
Death	25
Bereavement	3
Supernatural	20
Hope	9
Deep emotion	7
Self-denial	6
Embraces	4
Pathos	4
Horror	2
Comedy	12
Abstract	2
Nature	1

The emphasis on supernatural endings is striking: 20 per cent of the votes were cast for fade-outs with the spirits of the dead living happily in the other world though they could not do so in this. It was not possible to ascertain precisely how many films have such endings, but a random survey of 100 did not reveal a single one, and further investigation unearthed only one not mentioned in the competition, which dated back to silent days.

Of the first fifteen films on the list, over half were more than three years old at the time, which shows that the memories have stuck and are not just a random collection of endings which happen to have struck people in the immediate past. Moreover, the ones with a supernatural ending were among the oldest. *Three Comrades* was made in 1938; *A Tale of Two Cities* in 1935. *Lost Horizon*, which deals with what may be described as a heaven on earth, was made in 1937. *Smiling Through*, the whole theme of which is communication between the dead and the living, was made in 1932; it came ninth on the list.[1]

The popularity of endings bears no relationship to the frequency with which such themes occur; strikingly the reverse. For instance nearly 40 per cent of both men and

[1] It is perhaps worth noticing that there are no signs that the entrants for this competition were in any sense "highbrow" or people particularly interested in cinema. Apart from the fact that the competition was run by

women mentioned tragic fade-outs, but a random sample of 100 films contained only twelve tragedies, and of these twelve only two had tragic endings. Supernatural themes and endings which turn out to make such an impression are even rarer.

How are we to interpret these findings in view of the evidence given earlier in this chapter? We suggest that, whatever else the confusion of ideas demonstrated may imply, it cannot be taken as meaning simple lack of interest. People are *not* content to pass over the question of life after death as unimportant and see life simply as a matter of making the best of this world. Very many are unable to accept the idea of an afterlife, but that does not mean that they are content to reject it. The desire remains. Hollywood's heaven and her spirits of the departed fill a gap, and it is questionable whether the gap is better filled than it was with its original contents.

In recent months there have been a considerable number of films made with other-world sequences as an essential part of the story. *The Song of Bernadette*, in which Bernadette sees the Virgin Mary and is able to work miracles; *A Guy named Joe*, in which the ghosts of dead airmen work with live ones and control them; *The Uninvited*, in which the ghosts of past occupants of a house have to be exorcised; *Halfway House*, in which a ghost with a ghost staff returns to earth to guide the living; *Between Two Worlds*, a remake of *Outward Bound*, which failed to obtain the Censor's certificate, showing men and women on their way to another world. Leaving out the purely comic ghost, or the simply terrifying, there have been numerous supernatural settings, of which *Blithe Spirit* is a borderline case—perhaps it would be stretching a point to suggest that some people might "get something" other than a laugh out of this? Bing Crosby has played the part of a priest in a film with no real love story; the occupied-country thriller *Till We Meet Again* has a nun as heroine.

The reverse side of this picture is the apparent decline in the output of scientific thrillers. The pseudo-scientific film,

a popular Sunday paper, there is additional evidence in the fact that films with an obvious social content are scarcely mentioned. The only exception was *Blockade*, which ends with an impassioned speech on the idiocy of war and was mentioned nine times. There is every reasonable indication that these are ordinary film-goers.

with its implicit moral that anything is possible in the laboratory, making midget men or monsters, bringing the dead to life, changing people's brains around—and its implicit emphasis on the non-necessity of the supernatural—appears at present to have practically disappeared. Boris Karloff and Bela Lugosi are no longer playing the part of mad scientists.

By and large, makers of films are conservative. People will go and see the stars long after the theme has begun to pall, and the box-office index lags behind the first real changes in taste. A new theme, to be an immediate success, needs an audience which is ready for it. So far as film themes bear a relation to public taste, they are more likely to reflect it than create it. Like the newspaper Press, they reinforce and bring into the open what is already there; confirm and strengthen, rather than change and create. Reflected in the current trend towards supernatural themes and the disappearnace of the omnipotent scientist (who does God's job, though usually with a hitch), we can see very much the pattern of what is going on in people's minds. Science is not omnipotent as it seemed to be once; Heaven is not what people were brought up to believe it was like; science has made people reject the old ideas of Heaven and afterlife, so let science produce a new Heaven and a new afterlife—something to believe in beyond science, because science isn't infallible, after all.

Significantly, the psychiatrist and mental expert has taken the place of the materialist laborarory magician. But he is no longer infallible.

In *Dead of Night*, after he has debunked the allegedly supernatural experiences of half a dozen obviously very sane people, he persuades the last not to run away from his feeling that he has "been here before" in a dream—and that unnamed disaster is going to occur if he stays. The dreamer stays, sweating with apprehension, against his "better judgment," with no idea as to what is about to happen. Then, relentlessly and predestinedly, he murders the scientist—for no "reason" at all.

This theme may be compared with the prototype of robot stories, Capek's *R.U.R.* In *R.U.R.*, the robots also kill their makers, but it is not so much the makers' fault that things come to this pass as the fault of one of their wives. There is a "deliberate mistake," outside the scientist's control; the tacit assumption that all *could* have gone to plan if human-nature had not intervened. But the *Dead of Night* scientist has the situation completely under his control, his subject behaves according to his wishes to the letter. There is no ambiguity about what killed him; it was the limitations of his own scientific outlook. Alternatively, and amounting to much the same thing, there is Nigel Balchin's treatment of the psychiatric theme in his novel, *Mine Own Executioner*. Here the subject of psychiatric treatment kills his wife, and himself. Physically, the psychiatrist is unscathed, but since his solution to the problem presented to him is to give up his work as a psychiatrist, he may be presumed dead as a *scientist*. On the last page he changes his mind, but the reader is left wondering whether the same pattern will not repeat itself in the future.

The theme which is coming to the fore now in drama and literature is a rejection of reason as the mainstay of life. It appears in Thornton Wilder's play, *The Skin of Our Teeth*, in W. H. Auden's *For the Time Being*, most clearly in Ronald Duncan's *This Way to the Tomb*. Priest and scientist combine in the latter play in Father Opine, television parson of the future, leading his Astral Group round the world in helicopters, debunking miracles. (He announces himself in Basic English: "Good ones, this is Father Thought to spoke.") The Group chants as they dance to a Slow Waltz, their creed, beginning:

> *Above man is thought*
> *Below man is material*
> *Man is the centre*
> *We believe in Man*
> *In his mind's effort*
> *And his modest plan.*

And the Chorus, observing the proceedings, puts the question which is the dilemma that the play presents:

> *Can no one stop this garrulous crusade*
> *Before it converts us all to doubt,*
> *And desecrates the Trinity,*

Taking the square root of Faith
And hands us relativity?
Oh how the deserts of the heart contract
Watered by dryness and confounded fact?

There is a Resurrection in this play, another in Emlyn Williams' *The Wind of Heaven*. W. H. Auden, following the Christ-theme and saturated in *The Tempest*, has so far stopped short of resurrection and failed to follow Shakespeare into his latest period. But the whole atmosphere of *For the Time Being* is one of anticipation of revelation.

Meantime, more and more of the ex-rationalist wing are falling into very rational doubt about reason-without-ethics, ethics-without-sanction. Koestler, who dispassionately documented totalitarian reason in *Darkness at Noon*, moved on to Yogi. Compare the Heard-Huxley school—[1]

"The next step is to realise that civilisation's crisis is a consequence of a crisis in thought. Men are not behaving irrationally; they are behaving violently; but the violence is due to their acting on certain arguments. It was Reason which told them they could not behave otherwise than violently, and so they are following Reason"

and George Orwell, now brilliantly pursuing the original Koestler theme, the development of reason-without-ethics in a totalitarian State:[2]

"A totalitarian society which succeeded in perpetuating itself would probably set up a schizophrenic system of thought, in which the laws of common sense held good in everyday life and in certain exact sciences, but could be disregarded by the politician, the historian and the sociologist."

Koestler, in the meantime, seems to have swung back to the rational justification of violence, for the old humanitarian ends (see his latest book, *Thieves in the Night*). And, at the mass level, *Psychic News*, with a circulation (28,000) of which any political weekly would be proud, has as its boxed slogan on each issue: "LIFE AFTER DEATH *PROVED*."

[1] Gerald Heard, *The Third Morality*.
[2] George Orwell, *The Prevention of Literature* (*Polemic*, January 2nd, 1946).

VI

ORTHODOXY

WE HAVE ALREADY SAID enough to show that people's ideas about religion deviate very widely, even among churchgoers, from the orthodox dogma of the Church. This is particularly true of those attached to the Church of England, less so of Nonconformists, and much less so of Roman Catholics. The latter group we consider later: there were not enough Nonconformists in the sample for any but the broadest generalisations to be possible. For the moment, we confine our attention to Church of England churchgoers.

The Divinity of Christ

Two further points were investigated as a rough test of orthodoxy—belief in the divinity of Christ, and in the Virgin Birth. People were first asked whether they thought that Christ was just a man, or whether He was something more than that.

Forty-four per cent. of men and 60 per cent. of women said they thought He was more than a man; 38 per cent. of men and 21 per cent. of women that He was "only a man," the rest being undecided or uninterested. The more educated were more able to give a definite opinion, but their opinions were distributed in the same way as those of the less educated. In all, just over half the people of Metrop tend to believe in the divinity of Christ.

If we now correlate belief in the divinity of Christ with belief in a Deity and with churchgoing, we find:[1]

Attitude to Divinity of Christ	Believe in God	Don't believe in God	Go to Church of England Services	Don't go to Church
Believe	61	25	55	41
Do not believe	25	53	27	37
Undecided, uninterested	14	32	18	22

Percentage expressing this Attitude among Those who say they—

[1] Those who say that Christ was an "extraordinary man" are classified here as believing in His divinity.

Thus, a quarter of Church of England churchgoers, and about the same proportion of those who believe in a Deity do not believe in the divinity of Christ. Conversely, a quarter of those who have no definite belief in a Deity tend to believe in the divinity of Christ; and two-fifths of those who don't go to Church say they think Christ was "more than a man."

Virgin Birth

People were then asked whether they thought Christ was born of a Virgin Mother or not.

One woman in every four and more than two men in five said they did not believe in the Virgin Birth, and only about one person in three was really definite in saying they believed.

If we include the vague ones as believers, among younger people 38 per cent. believe, compared with 51 per cent. of the older generation.

The more educated are the most often sceptical, though they are no more able to give an opinion than the less educated.

Breaking down the results by belief in God and churchgoing, we find:

Attitude to Virgin Birth	Believe in God	Do not believe in God	Go to Church of England Services	Do not go to Church
Believe	56	16	56	30
Disbelieve	25	58	25	44
Undecided, uninterested	19	26	19	26

The figures for those who attend Church of England services and those who express some sort of belief in a Deity are identical in this instance; in both cases one-quarter disbelieve in the doctrine of the Virgin Birth. Conversely, one in six of those who doubt or deny the existence of a Deity believe that Christ was born of a virgin.

One further point is worth comment. If we relate people's expressed beliefs about the divinity of Christ to their attitude towards the doctrine of the virgin birth, we find that:

> 19 per cent. of those who say definitely that they think Christ was only a man also say definitely that they think He was born of a virgin.

16 per cent. of those who say definitely that they think Christ was more than a man also say definitely that they think he was *not* born of a virgin.

Unorthodoxy

The points of orthodoxy which we have discussed concern:

> (a) Belief in an afterlife.
> (b) Belief in the divinity of Christ.
> (c) Belief in the Virgin Birth.

Less than one-third of Metrop people say they have been to any sort of Church service during the past six months.[1] Of those who have attended a Church of England service in this period:

46 per cent. disbelieve or are undecided about whether there is any life after death.

45 per cent. disbelieve or are undecided about whether Christ was something "more than a man."

44 per cent. disbelieve or are undecided about whether Christ was born of a virgin.

A not very rigid test of orthodoxy may be devised to include those who believe in all three of these points and believe in the existence of a Deity. Less than one-third of those who have been to a Church of England service in the past six months pass this test.

It may be objected that it is unfair to include the undecided with those who definitely disbelieve in this way—indecision might be due to inarticulateness rather than a real lack of belief. The replies of Roman Catholics, however, suggest that this is not the case. Four Roman Catholics out of five gave definite affirmative replies to *all* these questions; so, too, did two out of three Nonconformists. None of the Catholic churchgoers were undecided about the divinity of Jesus or about the Virgin Birth, and, as we shall see later, this definiteness of viewpoint among Catholics was found on other questions as well. There is no reason why Catholics should be more articulate than others by nature, and we can legitimately

[1] Almost certainly an overestimate: cf. next chapter.

assume that indecision is due to a confused attitude rather than lack of self-expression.

What is Orthodox?

Verbatim comments showed that many people were far from clear what *was* the orthodox thing to believe about the divinity of Christ. In framing this question, we were faced with the double difficulty of putting a complex idea into universally comprehensible words, and of avoiding words with an emotional content which would lead people to reply in a particular way. After considerable experimenting, the phrasing finally adopted was: "Do you think that Jesus Christ was just a man or something more than that?" The replies of those who mentioned the teachings of the Bible or the Church ranged over the following scale:

"According to the Bible, He was only a man, and we've only got that to go by" (M45 El).

"I can't see how He could have been more than a man. He was supposed to be a man, wasn't He?" (M60 El).

"Well, according to what we read in the Bible, He was just a superman" (M60 El).

"Well, I don't know. Something more than an ordinary man. So the Bible says" (M50 El).

"Well, according to what we've been taught, He was certainly more than a man, and when you read all the things He did in the Bible, He was obviously more than a man" (F30 El).

Those who say that Christ was only a man are thus not necessarily refuting what they understand to be the teachings of Christianity. On the other hand, there were many, especially among young people, who replied in this vein:

"Oh, I've read it all through, and I think that Jesus was just a man. Quite a good chap" (M20 Sec).

"Well, He was just a human being, just like we" (M35 Sec).

"Well, I don't think He was anything extra. No superman" (M30 El).

The wording of several replies suggested that, though the people concerned believed that Christ must have been something more than a man if the Gospel story is true, they were not entirely convinced that it was:

"Well, I don't know. What you're taught sticks in your mind. I suppose He was more than a man really. All those miracles. If they were true" (F25 Sec).

"Well, if it's true what we're told and what we believe, He was more than a man" (M50 El).

Several people doubted whether Christ had ever lived:

"Not sure whether I believe that he actually lived or not" (F30 Sec).

"I don't think he was either. I think he was just a romance of the imagination. In somebody's mind" (M50 El).

These comments, though not frequent, were made often enough to show that a not insignificant proportion of ordinary people nowadays believe Christ to be a mythological figure:

"Only a man. That's if He ever was at all. He may have been something like Father Christmas" (F45 El).

"Well, sometimes I get the belief that Jesus Christ was a myth, but put to us by the so-called Christians more or less to civilise the world" (M55 El).

"I reckon He never existed. It's just a sort of fairy tale" (M20 El).

A few, though they did not think Christ an entirely fictional character, doubted whether the gospel versions of his life were accurate:

"Well, it's hard to believe when you get a book so old as that, it may be exaggerated. It may be exaggerated from a man, especially as it's translated. So much is definitely not true in some places" (M20 El).

There were also a variety of "explanations" of Christ:

"I don't know. Was there ever a Jesus Christ? Take some of our surgeons to-day; they do such clever things that they're almost miracles in themselves" (F30 El).

"Oh no. Just a man. This may sound strange to you, but if Hitler had won the war he would have been a second Jesus Christ. If he'd have done well, it would have been Germany would have ruled the world, and only German people left, and it would have been told their children and their children's children that Hitler was a second Christ and Goering and Goebbels and those were his disciples. He would have been what Jesus was for good—world-famous—only it wouldn't have been for good" (F30 El).

A sixty-year-old carpenter, who had clearly thought the matter over carefully, said:

"I don't doubt He existed. He was a carpenter, same as myself. And I've come to the conclusion years ago that He must have been too lazy to work, because to be a carpenter in those days must have been hard work. He must have read and studied at the bench, and all the rest is pure invention. Most people at that time were ignorant, and they lived far apart, and in a very primitive way, and He was able to influence the illiterate, and the people invented He was something holy" (M60 El).

And a young apprentice:

"No, I think Jesus Christ was a lady. Don't you think so?" (M17 Sec).

Such is the diversity of unorthodox opinion on the question of the nature of Christ. Opinions were not a great deal less mixed among Church of England churchgoers than they were among the population of Metrop as a whole. But of the forty-two Catholic churchgoers included in the sample only one said he thought that Christ was just a man.

On the question of the Virgin Birth, there were many who rejected the idea as a simple fabrication. These included several who nevertheless believed in Christ's divinity, and a considerable minority of Church of England people. Two churchgoers said:

"Well, I don't know about that. I should think that's a bit of a fairy tale added by the clergy" (F45 Sec).

"I don't think so. It seems rather . . . She's supposed to have had a husband, isn't she? Joseph (F30 Sec).

The following were typical of the more sceptical comments:

"That's a stroke to come over with. Well, I don't know. I've a single girl, and wouldn't like her to put that one over me. I wonder how I'd feel; that's how I look at it. That is a query" (F45 El).

"No definitely not. I've never seen a virgin give birth yet" (M35 El).

"It's hard to believe. A spirit with a virgin and a man as a result. It's rather hard" (M30 Sec).

"No. I don't. You don't expect me to believe that. I'm having a baby and that's no miracle" (F30 El).

"Now, as a woman, I've had three children myself, and I don't see how she can have been a virgin. These things get past me" (F40 El).

"No, it's against all rules and regulations" (F25 El).

"Now you're asking me. That's something to swallow. If my wife came home with that tale, I'd tell her the Holy Ghost could keep it too" (M70 El).

Many rejected the idea on such grounds of personal experience, and, though unqualified rejection was no more frequent than on the question of Christ's divinity, it tended to be more outright and outspoken. There were, however, more qualified replies than on the former point. This is partly accounted for by the fact that some people are half-clinging to a belief they were brought up on, but can no longer wholly accept:

"I was always taught to believe it. That's what I've got against religion—that they teach you to believe things your reason can't accept, but it's very hard to shake them off in later life" (F30 Sec).

"Well, you can't really say. It's what you were brought up with at school" (F30 El).

"I believe in miracles, but I'm not too sure about that" (F30 El).

"It says born unto the Virgin Mary, yet somehow I can't believe it. I think He was just put there" (F30 El).

As one old man remarked: "There's so many things for and so many against. There's some grand comical things happen at times." But most of those who look on it this way quite naturally decide against. To look in the present for a parallel, for some unprecedented and inexplicable happening on which to base a faith in past miracles, is a forlorn quest. The grand comical thing does not happen in the modern and reasonable city, and when it seems to have done so, the next day's newspaper affably explains it away.

Yet it is the essence of contemporary scepticism that people are looking for parallels on which to build a creed. They won't take the past and its beliefs on trust, and unless they can see history's reflection in the present, history is bunk.

The Virgin Birth may or may not be an important part of dogma; the divinity of Christ may or may not be an essential tenet of Christianity. But both beliefs have a long history of orthodoxy, of stable acceptance for many generations. They have been, to some extent, outside the bounds of ordinary conversational debate. What, to-day, one Metrop citizen in four will say publicly and without qualms would, in many cases, have created a profound shock if it had been said in the privacy of the home by his father or his grandfather. In one sense, no doubt, the change is for the best. The area of *tabu* is shrinking. There are steadily fewer things it isn't done to talk about, to admit questioning. Ostensibly, at any rate, minds are being cleared. But are they? If Christ was just a man, and Mary just a wife, if God is a likely probability and life after death a less likely one, then it is sensible enough not to trouble too much about these things. But if, in crises, the people who don't bother about God start praying to Him; if, at funerals, the people who don't bother about life after death want assurance; if, some Sundays, the people who don't bother about the details and think some of them are inaccurate, attend services at which they say, "I believe . . ." knowing that they are, at the least, very doubtful—then we may legitimately be suspicious. Are these minds clearer, or are they in fact less clear than ever?

VII

CHURCHGOING

THE QUESTION OF CHURCHGOING is one on which it is very difficult to obtain accurate data. There is a certain prestige value attached to *saying* one goes to church, even if one has not been for many months or hardly at all for several years. Various bodies have on occasion asked people questions about their churchgoing habits which have produced figures that are known to be too high, and have, on a local scale, been checked against actual church attendances. While there is a tendency for those who *ever* attend church to exaggerate the frequency with which they go, an overall figure of fair accuracy for those who never attend at all, except on special occasions, such as funerals and weddings, can be obtained. In Metrop, people were asked whether they ever went to church; and, if they said they did, they were asked when was the last time they went. Just how all-embracing this first question is was illustrated by the reply of one man who said he did go to church; but when asked for the approximate date of his last attendance could recall no visit since church parade in the 1914–18 War. Having said that they do go to church, there is clearly going to be a tendency for people to justify their statement by naming a date in the not-too-distant past, and in all that follows we are likely to be giving an over-estimate of the real facts about churchgoing.

In Metrop, 61 per cent. of people *say* they never go to church, or only go for funerals and such occasions. The remainder consist of:

24 per cent. who say they go to Church of England services.
8 per cent. who say they go to Roman Catholic services.
6 per cent. who say they go to Nonconformist services.
1 per cent. who say they go to Jewish services.

If we eliminate from this 39 per cent. of churchgoers those who *admit* later that they haven't been to church for the past six months, the proportion is reduced to 28 per cent., and of this minority:

> Rather over a third say they last went up to one week ago.
> Rather less than a third say they last went between a week and a month ago.
> A third say they last went over a month, and up to six months, ago.

Taking the date of their last visit is a considerably more reliable method of finding the frequency with which people go to church than asking them to give their own estimate, but even then we have to allow for a tendency to give a more recent date than the actual one. The most we can deduce from these figures is that, at the very outside, *about one person in ten in Metrop goes to church fairly regularly*, and another two go at intervals ranging upwards to once a year.

There have been to church during the past six months:

> Less than a quarter of men.
> About a third of women.
> Less than a quarter of young people.
> One-third of old people.
> Practically identical proportions of more and less educated people.

Not only do fewer men than women go to church at all, but those who do go, go less frequently.

> Of men churchgoers, only a quarter have been within the week (i.e. about one in twenty of Metrop men).
> Of women churchgoers, nearly half have been within the week (i.e. about one in seven of all Metrop women).

Hence, one would expect the congregations of Metrop churches on an ordinary Sunday to consist of about three-quarters women. Actual counts made at various London churches do, in fact, show this to be about the normal distribution.

Though there are more non-churchgoers among young

people, those who do go to church go no less frequently than their elders. The proportions who have been within a week, a month, and six months are identical for young and old. On the other hand, though there is no difference between the proportions of more and less educated people who do not go to church at all, the more educated go much more regularly:

> Of churchgoers with secondary education, over half have been within the week.
> Of churchgoers with elementary education, less than a third have been within the week.

The Metrop churches on a given Sunday thus contain predominantly women, old people, educated people: and there is about one chance in ten of finding any citizen in church at some time during the day.

Churchgoing and Orthodoxy

The regular churchgoers and those who pass the test of orthodoxy detailed in the foregoing chapter are not all the same people, but they amount to about the same proportion of Metrop citizens. Actually, the proportion of people who have been to church within the past six months and hold orthodox views on the subjects mentioned is about one in seven, but if we are looking for some criterion of association with organised religion we can hardly include those who only go to church two or three times a year. A rough figure, derived, firstly, from regular churchgoing, and, secondly, from the possession of a minimum of clear orthodox views plus a less rigid test of Church observances, is 10 per cent. This proportion of Metrop people may be considered at all closely linked to the organised Churches. And that may well be an over-estimate because of the general human tendency to say the orthodox thing, if you know it and if your personal views are not pronounced.

VIII

PRAYER

NON-CHURCHGOERS WERE ASKED if they ever prayed, and churchgoers were asked if they prayed apart from in church.

Nearly three men out of five and more than one woman in five say they never pray outside. Identical proportions of the more and less educated say they pray. Young people less often pray than old people, though not outstandingly so.

Of those who say they believe in a Deity, a quarter say they never pray, or pray only in church; and precisely the same proportion of those who don't believe admit they *do* pray.

Of the people who go to Church of England services, about one in five admit they never pray except in church. But 98 per cent. of the Catholic churchgoers say they pray outside church.

Those who said they prayed were then asked if they would mind saying what they prayed about. The question was asked well on in the interview, when confidence had been established with the interviewee, and the majority were prepared to answer. Nevertheless, the results must clearly not be taken as giving any absolute measure of the content of private prayer. Their interest lies chiefly in the difference between the answers of the various groups.

Of the 214 people who answered this question:

34 per cent. mentioned prayers about their family and friends.

32 per cent. mentioned prayers to do with protection.

29 per cent. mentioned prayers about people in general, or special people other than their own acquaintances.

21 per cent. mentioned prayers about themselves.

16 per cent. mentioned prayers about crises.

3 per cent. mentioned other subjects of prayer.[1]

[1] Many people mentioned more than one subject or occasion of prayer, so that the percentages total over 100.

Clearly there is a tendency to claim to pray unselfishly, and for this reason the personal categories are not to be relied on. The classification was designed chiefly to compare the frequency of protection and crisis prayers in the different groups. "Crises" were taken to be exceptional difficulties such as might make pray those not used to prayer, rather than everyday difficulties. The analysis mixes the objects of prayer and the occasions of prayer, but this is simply a reflection of the way people look on it themselves—some generalising about *when* they pray, and some particularising about who they pray *for*. They were asked, however, what they prayed *about* and not *when* they prayed. It is of some significance that so many answered in terms of the state of mind which induced them to pray.

Six in ten of the prayers of those who doubt or deny the existence of God are crisis and protection prayers—compared with three in ten of those who say they believe in God.[1]

The Pattern of Prayer

Another investigation was also made among the National Panel of correspondents in which people discussed their private prayers in detail and more frankly than was possible in verbal interviewing. The general subject matter and occasions of prayer were much the same among this more "thinking" sample, though prayers for self were more often mentioned. This, however, probably reflects nothing more than the more anonymous nature of the investigation. In the following discussion material from both sources is considered.

Not a great deal need be said about the general subject-matter of prayer, since it is so close to the accepted pattern. "God bless Mummy and Daddy and keep the soldiers and sailors safe, and make me a good boy. And don't let that aeroplane drop a bomb"—this sort of childhood prayer covers all five of the main topics, and, sometimes not very much elaborated, constitutes the essential framework of much adult prayer. Sometimes, indeed, the prayers learnt in early

[1] Note that these latter figures are proportions of all prayers, not of people praying; the earlier figures referred to the proportion of people who include each subject among their prayers.

childhood are continued in almost the same words many years later. This came out clearly in the franker written replies. A housewife, for instance:

"I do not pray, not since I was a child, but at night I say to myself, 'Please God keep my Dad and Mum safe' (they are dead), and when sirens have sounded I find myself saying, 'Oh, God, stop this awful war before there's more damage and lives lost.'"

And a woman research worker of twenty-six:

"I have always said prayers before going to bed. This used to start with a formal bit, a sort of opening, then the part in the middle I was really interested in demanding sundry blessings and including favoured relatives, finishing up with 'Our Father.' For about the last six months I've left off the formal bit, cut down the list of relatives considerably (some of them have died and I never know whether to go on including them or not), and cut 'Our Father' off the end because I don't see what good it can do."

This is an intimate point which one would scarcely expect to show much in verbal interviews. There were, however, one or two remarks like the following, which showed a similar repetition of a formula whose implications had been forgotten, if they were ever known:

"I pray about nothing in particular. I just say the prayers I've said ever since I was a child. I don't know what one actually thinks when one's saying them" (F30 Sec).

The continuous, uncritical repetition of a rigmarole learnt in childhood may go on night after night for years, long after the mind has ceased to give conscious assent to the sentiments expressed. In the same way, a childhood belief in God, consciously discarded in workaday life, comes suddenly to the fore in crises and when the individual is unable to grapple with his own problems alone. The majority of the prayers of non-believers were of this nature; and it is significant that only a few of those who, a few minutes back, had said they weren't sure there was a God, showed by their comments that they felt it extraordinary to pray to Him under duress. The few who did make remarks like this:

"Quite frankly, I don't know what I'm praying to. I thank God when I'm tremendously happy. I thank God for coming through" (F35 Sec).

"People get weak-minded when they're scared stiff. I pray that we'll be spared. Then I think some other poor devil's getting it, and I add on a bit about *him*. You're not *reasonable* when the buzz-bombs are cutting out overhead" (M45 Sec).

Other typical comments from doubters and non-believers who pray occasionally give the general atmosphere:

"Mostly I pray when I'm frightened or worried about something" (F19 Sec).

"The last time I prayed was getting away from Dunkirk" (M35 El: says he disbelieves in God, thinks there is no afterlife, and never goes to church).

"Well perhaps I might have, once or twice when we had the doodle bugs around so much. You sort of say a little bit in spite of yourself, as it were. It's fetched out of you before you know" (M25 El: beliefs as M35 above).

"Not as a rule; only when I'm afraid and I need help. It doesn't sound very nice, does it. But I'm afraid I only pray when I need something" (M35 Sec).

"Oh, sometimes when I want anything. When you're indoors you say, 'I'll pray to God for this and that.' Just like asking for something. People's got different ideas. My mind might be different from other people's" (F35 El).

"Well, it's mostly if I'm afraid of anything. To keep the baby safe and that sort of thing" (F19 El).

Under physical and mental stress, about one in four of those who question or reject the existence of God admit that they pray to Him for help out of difficulty or danger. Doubtless, this is an under-estimate of the proportion of "disbelievers" who do, on occasion, pray. But that so many admit it is an indignation of the extent to which agnosticism and atheism fail to penetrate below the expressional, verbal surface. God is an uneasy bet in crisis to a large number of those for whom His existence or non-existence is of slight, everyday importance, and whose normal routine attitude is doubt or denial. The implied confusion may be illustrated by an extreme. A young man of nineteen, who says unequivocally, "No, I don't think there is a God," who says of life after death, "I think you just die and that's the end," who thinks Christ was just a man, who never goes to church—but:

"Well, I pray like for my brother in the Army, and in the Live Letter Column in the *Daily Mirror* people in their letters ask for your help, and so I pray for them. I have done if their letter appeals."

Pray to whom?

Believers Pray

But the crisis and protection prayer punctuating long intervals of non-prayer is by no means confined to those who question the existence of God. Many of the believers pray only on such special occasions. The main difference is that their prayers are more often made in *mental* rather than physical crisis:

"Well, I do when I think I've got more trouble than I can handle. But it's got to be something very bad to make me pray" (F55 El).
"There was a time when I thought I was going blind, couldn't see at all with one eye, and I used to pray to save my eyes. While the war is on the mind goes to God to see if He can't turn it round the other way" (M70 El).
"When I'm pushed and can't do for myself, I ask someone to help me" (M60 El).
"Well, not what you'd call praying. Only if I'm terror-stricken or a bomb's falling near" (M60 El).
"Sometimes I get so down it gets the better of me, and then I pray for courage to work for my little girl and keep her decent" (F35 El).

"Only when I lose my temper" (M55 El).

"Well, I do when I've got an exam" (M20 El).

"I ask if I've any worries to be relieved of them, or if the family is ill I ask God to make them better" (F40 El).

"Yes, during the blitz, when things were bad, I prayed to relieve my feelings. Not help—just nerves more than anything else" (M18 El).

There was a considerable amount of spontaneous comment against the idea that prayer involved kneeling down:

"Well, I do pray now and again, about any little thing that worries me, and I pray inside myself, not kneeling down or anything like that, pretty well every time the warning goes" (F25 Sec).

"Well, now, what is praying? I don't go down on my hands and knees, if that's what you mean. Going down on your hands and knees isn't praying. You can lie in bed and pray" (M55 El).

The interpretation of these comments is debatable, but it seems probable that frequent protests against praying in the formal way indicate much the same reaction against ritual as the protests against churchgoing which we shall discuss later. But those believers who welcome the decline in formal religious observances as a decline in hypocrisy (an attitude which is often implicit) should not overlook the fact that current informalism may, on occasion, be very difficult to distinguish from straight superstition. As one old man said:

"Well, I pray about all sorts of things. About my son being away and different family troubles, not my own. . . . *Thinking a lot is as good as praying. It's wishing. Wishing's the same as praying. Wishing is only a way of asking*" (M55 El).

In assessing the validity of the above, we have to bear in mind two factors:

(*a*) That there is likely to be a strong incentive for those who have already said they believe—and particularly for those who go to church—to *say* that they pray privately.

The fact that one in four say they don't ever, and that many more admit that they pray only in periods of danger, crisis and worry, shows clearly that habitual private prayer is rare to-day, even among believers.

(*b*) On the other hand, there would be a strong incentive for those who say they doubt or deny the existence of a God to *say* they never pray. The fact that one in four of these admit that they do pray shows that sporadic prayer is very common, even among disbelievers.

The general picture we are left with is one of a great volume of special pleas addressed erratically to the Deity, in which the voices of believers and disbelievers mingle in anxiety, fear and inability to grapple alone; punctuated by long periods of relative quiet when the workaday world presents fewer humanly insoluble problems and humanly insurmountable dangers. In these periods, a thinner stream of private problems from believers and disbelievers unable to find a solution alone, and the voices of the small band of regular prayers.

During the Blitz a hymn was composed and set to music, which was sent to Mass-Observation from various parts of the country as a specimen of wartime literature. It began:

> *God is our refuge, be not afraid,*
> *He will be with you all through the raid.*

And it included this sentiment:

> *When bombs are dropping and danger is near,*
> *He will be with you, until the all clear.*

And after the All Clear? There are few overt signs to-day that the refugees to God are acquiring a new or revived faith through these brief and repeated moments of appeal. There may be a long-term effect which is not yet discernible on the surface, but if so, there is no *a priori* reason for supposing it will emerge as religious revival. Something from the more distant past may be revived, or something quite different may be substituted.

We may compare the ups and downs of crisis prayer with the ups and downs of belief in astrology. Mass-Observation has made a number of investigations at various periods during the war of the extent to which people admit they believe at all in astrology. In 1941 somewhere around 40-50 per cent. said they had some belief in it; in the first half of 1942 it was about 30–35 per cent.; later in the year it was in the twenties; and since then it has been in the teens. The pattern is fairly clear. Till the entry of Russia into the war, the future was a matter for faith. When it became clear that Russia was going to resist, it became more reasonable to suppose that the future might be looked after by man's efforts. Since then it has become increasingly probable that the future will work out all right without astral intervention, or rather without malign and benign influences turning events away from the logical, reasonable-looking sequence. When a drowning man clutches at a straw and saves himself, he does not believe that he needs a straw to sustain and uphold his future life. The straw has its momentary importance, but when the crisis is past it is just a straw again. In the prayers which people have made while they were in danger or in trouble during this war, there is no more sign of religious revival than there is of astrological revival in the facts here outlined. That people have turned temporarily to astrology when they can't see the way out is in itself a symptom suggestive of the meaning and depth of crisis prayer. It is an uneasy gamble when the logic of events seems to point inevitably in the wrong direction, and a long chance seems the only chance. But afterwards "reason" regains her former status, attitudes revert to *status quo*.

Whether this is a good or a bad thing, whether the prevalence of doubt of an at least superficially "rational" kind is to be welcomed, or whether it represents an application of reason to the wrong object (a denial by reason of something superior to reason), it is not within the province of this report to discuss. These crisis prayers show the need of people for something to which to appeal, a need filled in many cases by something which, in their less desperate moments, they reject, or ignore. This need has been brought to people's attention particularly by the human desperations of war. It has been filled by prayer and it has been filled by newspaper astrology. But neither have proved so satisfactory that people have kept allegiance when the crisis has passed. For increasingly many there is nothing stable outside themselves to call upon. Does this imply that people are becoming, or will become, increasingly self-sufficient? Or does it imply that in a new period of human difficulty they will be ready to accept some more reasonable-seeming substitute for the things to which they now appeal for help in crisis? A human being, an ideology, a down-to-the-ground, up-to-the-minute person or idea? These are the potential fillings for the great blank in workaday faith to-day. There is no very good reason to suppose that they will be judged much more critically than the newspaper astrologers if they come to the fore, as they well may do, in time of crisis and difficulty. But they may have more staying power, more potent machinery for seeing to it that they retain the faith once they gain it.

IX

CHRIST'S TEACHING AND THE TEN COMMANDMENTS

PEOPLE WERE ASKED what they thought of the life and teachings of Christ. This question was particularly interesting in the extent to which it showed trends of attitude among believers and non-believers, churchgoers and non-churchgoers, which were independent of age and sex factors.

The majority of both sexes replied favourably, and about a quarter of each sex had nothing to say at all. Definite criticism came from one man in eight, one woman in twenty.

However, there was no difference between the extent to which young and old, more and less educated, either criticised or qualified their admiration. The differences in the attitudes of those who do, and don't, believe in God are thus not a reflection of age or education. The figures show that they reflect considerably more than sex differences.

Thus, non-believers were critical three times as frequently as believers (15 per cent. to 5 per cent.) and only a third of non-believers gave *unqualified* praise to Christ's life and teachings—compared with two-thirds of believers.

The proportions of various groups who adopted critical or not whole adulatory attitudes were as follows:

Men, 25%. Young, 18%. Secondary Education, 19%.

Women, 12%. Old, 18%. Elementary Education, 18%.

And, by belief and practice, ranged in order of frequency:

Group	Percentage of this Group who criticise or give Qualified Praise to Life and Teachings of Christ
Roman Catholic churchgoers	7
Those who believe in Christ's divinity	11
Believers in God	13
Church of England churchgoers	16
Non-churchgoers	21
Those uncertain about divinity of Christ	24
Those who believe Christ was "only a man"	26
Non-believers in God	30

Though there was only a very slight difference by age, sex and education in the extent to which people were unable to offer any opinion, there were major differences when results were broken down by other religious attitudes and practices. Thus, in the first four groups enumerated above the proportion who were undecided or offered no opinion ranged from 10 per cent. (of Roman Catholics) to 21 per cent. (of believers in God). In the four latter groups it ranged from 29 per cent. (of non-believers in Christ's divinity) to 49 per cent. (of those uncertain about His divinity).

Though it is not quite so simple as this, it is roughly true to say that the people most critical of Christ's life and teachings are found in the groups least informed and opinionated about it. Criticism comes chiefly from the more uninterested groups, though a much more elaborate investigation would be necessary before it could be reliably suggested that criticism is related to ignorance. However, the pattern is an unusual one. In opinion questions it is most usual to find the less opinionated groups also the more accepting, whereas in this instance the opposite is the case. There is some ground for supposing that a qualified acceptance of Christ's example goes with ignorance of His life and teaching—certainly the survey gives no grounds for supposing that rejection and criticism are, in the main, a considered thing based on acquaintance with His teachings.

The outstanding point, however, is that only four people out of fifty were definitely critical, and even among non-believers and those who do not believe in Christ's divinity, less than one in seven adopted an attitude which seemed primarily critical.

Moreover, the great majority of all critical comments boiled down to saying that Christ's teachings and life were too perfect, too good to live up to, too idealistic. They differed in degree but not in kind from those which we have called "qualified praise." Very few people indeed said they *disagreed* with His teachings or did not admire His life, the nearest approaches being remarks of this kind:

> "Well, I think His life and teaching wants a lot of beating. There are one or two flaws in it: 'Give to him that asketh thee,' and you wouldn't have anything left. But generally it's a good conduct of life" (M70 El).
>
> "I think they're so impossible, one just has to dismiss them. Didn't he say, 'Be ye perfect' or something like that? Well, that's just ridiculous" (M35 Sec).

Typical comments from those who said His example was too hard to live up to:

> "They're too hard for the average person to follow. If people profess to follow them, they're mostly hypocrites because they can't be lived up to, and then they act as an argument for other people against going to Church or practising Christianity" (M50 Sec).
>
> "Well, if anyone could live up to them, perfect, but we're not built that way" (M50 Sec).
>
> "I wouldn't mind being like Him, but He was too good though" (F30 El).

There were many people, believers and non-believers, who said the world would be a better place if people lived up to Christ's teachings:

> "Personally, if they were really carried out, it would be a better world" (M20 Sec).
>
> "Well, I don't know; if we all acted up to them, the world wouldn't be at one another so" (M45 El).
>
> "I think He suffered, and that's why we suffer. And if we followed His teaching, we wouldn't have wars, because He teaches us to love one another" (M40 Sec).

Non-believers, as they did on the more general questions about religious belief, often said they thought Christ's teachings were excellent for other people who believed in them:

"I think His preachings have done a lot of good for those who believe in that sort of thing" (M55 El).

"Fine thing for those that thoroughly believe in them" (M30 Sec).

"Very good for the sort of people who want to believe it. And in uncivilised countries it's a good thing to bring to people who can't think of right. In countries like China and India, the uncivilised races" (F20 Sec).

Similarly, there were occasional people who said it was a good thing to believe in Christ's teaching even if Christ never existed:

"Well, I think they're very good. I think out of all His teaching, even if He wasn't real, you could always build something around what He said. However old they are, you can always turn them round to suit yourself" (M20 El).

Criticism of the Churches and of those who practise religious observances was again frequent, people saying that it was not the teachings that were wrong, but the uses to which they were put:

"They've been taken up by the wrong sort. If decent ordinary people were Christians the same as in His lifetime, well, there'd be more Christians in the world to-day. It's the sort that go to church that keep the rest away" (M45 Sec).

"Christ's teachings are what every man should live up to. It's not His teachings are the hindrance to Christianity to-day. Where is the hindrance is the trouble made by narrow-minded, bigoted people that find fault with others and can't live up to them themselves" (M50 El).

"I think they're very good—not doing evil to others and all that. But I think it was wrong for the Churches to set up and make a packet of money out of them—I don't think that was the idea at all. *He* didn't make five thousand a year and go to live in a palace like these bishops and archbishops" (M25 El).

"I think they were very fine. It's what the Churches have made of them that I'm not in favour of" (M35 Sec).

Most people find little to criticise about Christ's life and teachings except that they are too idealistic or have been abused. The belief that they are "too good" for practical purposes goes with lack of religious faith, and it seems likely that it also goes with non-informedness and disinterest. There is extremely little criticism except on these grounds of non-practicality. In general, it is true to say that most people who ignore or reject Christ's teachings as a guide in the everyday life do so because they feel them too good rather than because they feel them at all bad. As three eighteen-year-old non-believers put it:

"I think He had good intentions. It's quite a good thing, and I believe in His ideals, but I don't like the Church goings-on."

"Far as I can make out, it was a very good life. If you followed it, you couldn't go far wrong."

"It seems He never thought about Himself, and if everybody thought the same way, we wouldn't have need to worry."

Thus, though often in a very vague way, the ethics and ideals of Christianity are still looked upon by most people as good, and right, and admirable. But with the decline of religious faith comes the tendency to think they are *too* good, ideals too high to attempt to live up to in everyday life.

The Commandments

When people were asked what they thought of the Ten Commandments, precisely the same trend appeared, but with a stronger emphasis on the impracticality of such a code of behaviour in everyday life to-day. Numerical results were:

Attitude to the Commandments:	Percentage expressing this Attitude among—	
	Men	Women
Praise	46	52
Qualified Praise	12	8
Criticism	12	8
Often broken	10	7
Forgotten them, never knew	12	12
No opinion	8	13

Men were a little more critical than women, but only slightly so. The only difference between old and young was that 10 per cent. more young people said they'd forgotten the Ten Commandments or never knew them, and 10 per cent. fewer praised them unqualifiedly. Educated people were a little more critical than the less educated.

Non-believers in God were just as opinionated on the subject of the Ten Commandments as believers. But they praised them without qualification less than half as often (56 per cent.— 25 per cent.), criticised them twice as often, and said they had forgotten them twice as often.

Non-believers are thus considerably more critical of, and considerably less informed about, the Ten Commandments. The difference in attitude between non-churchgoers and those who go to Church of England services was not great, and was one of degree rather than kind; churchgoers qualified their praise, while non-churchgoers were more positively critical. One in ten of Church of England churchgoers replied by saying that they had forgotten the Ten Commandments, but none of the Catholic churchgoers said this.

Critical attitudes and attitudes of qualified praise in this case fall into three merging groups:

(a) Those who think the commandments are out-of-date and inapplicable to-day.

(b) Those who think they are impracticable to-day.

(c) Those who think they are so widely ignored to-day that they have become meaningless.

The first group is comparatively small, and consists largely of people who instance "love thy neighbour" or "thou shalt not kill":

"Well, they're old-fashioned now. 'Thou shalt not kill.' What would happen to the war effort if people took any notice of them?" (M30 El).

"Well, look at that commandment, 'Love thy neighbour.' Try it out to-day, and it's impossible to love thy neighbour—say, the Japs and Germans. I therefore cannot believe in it" (M20 El).

"An awful lot of 'thou shalt nots,' most of which don't apply any longer" (M45 Sec).

In the second group came comments like:

"They should be modified. The aspect of life now is different to what it was only a quarter of a century ago, to say nothing of the times of Moses" (M60 El).

"They're all right, but they don't work. They'd be marvellous if they worked, but they don't. I've tried. I'd help any lame dog over a stile, but nobody's ever helped me" (F30 El).

"Well, the trouble about those is, you can keep them all one day in the week, but you can't keep them all every day; it wouldn't be human" (M30 El).

The largest group were those who say the Commandments are good, but no one takes any notice of them:

"They're very sound and very good. They tell you exactly what you should do if you follow them, but one never does" (F30 Sec).

"Well, nobody keeps them. I'd like to see everybody keep by them but nobody does these days" (F20 Sec).

"If they were obeyed, they'd be all right. They tell you not to steal, yet the prisons are full of people. I don't think we can adhere strictly to them" (M25 El).

"Well, I've often thought about them, but I can't get clear really. They've a good understanding, but it's hard to say isn't it? Thou shalt not kill. Thou shalt not covet thyself to thy neighbour's wife. I should think when people have an idea of having a good time, they should sit and think, with their husband's not at home and they pick up with someone else and start trouble" (F35 El).

"Some are right and some are not. It says, 'Do not covet thy neighbour's wife, or thy neighbour's husband,' but they do. And 'Do not steal,' but they do" (F50 El).

"Well, the Ten Commandments. They're being broken day in, day out. Actually they might as well not exist" (M35 El).

"Well, the Ten Commandments are all right. I'd like to add to them. I think they're good, but they're not carried out. I've broken every one except murder" (M40 Sec).

As in the case of Christ's life and teachings, most people who have anything to say on the subject, irrespective of their religious beliefs, think in a vague way that the commandments are "good." We have quoted examples of the various types of critical attitude. They are critical, not of the rightness of the commandments, but of their applicability to life as they see it to-day. They seem remote from everyday behaviour, and many feel that, right though they may be, they don't really apply nowadays. Talking of the Commandments, people spontaneously mention murder, theft, neighbourliness, covetousness (of wives and husbands, not goods and chattels), adultery—the last two more than any. No one spontaneously mentioned the First Commandment. Attention focuses on the legalistic aspect, and the aspect of everyday behaviour. Just as the example of Christ, though they admire it, seems to many people too remote from everyday practice to have any bearing on their own lives, so the Commandments seem so far removed from to-day's actions that they have little bearing too. The process which is going on is not so much one of rejection as a toning down, a glossing over, a lack of interest in ideals whose practical implications seem to bear so little relation to the realities and possibilities of life to-day. People are seldom critical in the sense of having an alternative to offer. But as religious faith is weakening, so the old religion-based standards are weakening too. Among non-believers, many take the negative point of view of two young men who said of the Ten Commandments:

"Well, I suppose they're all right. You couldn't say there was anything very definitely *wrong* with them."

"They're a set of laws that should be abided by, because there is nothing wrong with them when one reads them."

Here, perhaps, lies the crux of the matter. Most people feel in a vague way that there's nothing much *wrong* with the old standards. Yet many feel that they are unrealistic and out of touch with everyday problems. No alternative yardstick offers itself, and behaviour deviates from the old pattern without any real rationale at all. One necessary effect of this weakening of commonly-accepted standards is that people are becoming more "independent"—their standards of behaviour and their aims are more their own. In the following sections we see something of the direction in which this "independence" is running.

X

WHAT IS RELIGION?

IT SEEMS HARDLY FAIR TO ask people to say on the spur of the moment what they think is meant by some conception which has for generations been discussed by specialists who have failed to arrive at any simple or universally acceptable conclusion. Yet it is true that when a word or an idea is thrown up in conversation, it has its own meaning to those present, and the way they talk about it will be determined largely by this private meaning. The immediate private meaning may be on a very superficial level, in one sense. For instance, the person who, when he hears the word "religion" mentioned, spontaneously feels impelled to introduce a condemnation of churchgoers, does not "mean" churchgoing by the word "religion." But his ideas about religion in general are probably highly coloured by his feelings about churchgoers in particular. Churchgoers are the trees which obscure his view of the wood. That is his private emphasis, and in describing people's attitudes the conversation-emphasis is of considerable importance. Give people time to think things out, and they will, according to their own light, put first things first. Throw out an idea and invite immediate verbal comment, "first" things may not come out at all, but privately important things will come out first. By asking people in a verbal interview, we approach this "superficial" level of personal stress—the conversation angle—though we may be very far from people's considered opinions, beliefs, total attitudes. Their replies have meaning, and an important meaning, provided we realise at what level the assessment is being made, and interpret accordingly.

People answered the question as follows:[1]

[1] Some people give a reply falling into more than one category, so that percentages add to over 100.

Meaning of the Word "Religion"	Percentage saying this was the Meaning among					
	Men		Women		Both	
"Belief" and "Belief in God"	26		30		28	
Specific beliefs (e.g. "Christianity," etc.)	8	34	8	38	8	36
Doing good, etc.	12		17		15	
Other ethical conduct	9		8		8	
Churchgoing, formal religious observances	9	30	9	34	9	32
Anti-church outbursts	7		2		4	
Anti-religious outbursts	10		3		7	
"Church not necessary"	3	20	4	9	3	14
Other comments	7		4		5	
Don't know	17		28		22	

In other words:

36 per cent. spontaneously define religion in terms of beliefs, faith and God.

32 per cent. spontaneously define it in terms of conduct.

14 per cent. spontaneously define it by criticising it.

And the rest are mostly unable to define it.

The first group need not detain us long. For the most part, they say simply that religion means believing in God, or "what you believe." Nearly a quarter of this group say that it means belief in Christ or in some specific sectarian creed; but this is more a difficulty of self-expression than a difference in conception.

Religion—Behaviour

The second large group are those who think of religion in terms of behaviour, and of these the largest sub-group think of it as doing good, being kind, helping others. While the majority would, if asked, no doubt say that belief in a Deity was essential to religion, some wouldn't. As one man said:

"Religion really . . . if a man's religious he may or may not have a creed. I say do all the good you can. Give everyone a square deal. There are very few really religious people about" (M55 El).

Typical comments included:

"Well, if people go through the world doing all they can in the way of good, it's as good a religion as any" (M35 Sec.: doubts existence of God; never prays; never goes to church).
"Well, to be good. Good as you possibly can be" (M80 El).
"Proper religion is to do what good you can" (M55 El).
"Doing good, in my opinion" (F25 El: doubts existence of God; never prays, never goes to church).

Others said religion meant being kind and helpful:

"To try and help each other as much as you would like help" (F20 El).
"My idea is being good to each other and helping those in trouble" (F35 El).
"My view is more or less help everyone as much as possible. It more or less covers everything" (M35 El).
"Doing anybody a good turn" (F50 El).
"Well, I think myself it's doing the best you can and being nice and kind. I don't know that all this praying is necessary to follow religion" (F40 El).
"A business; that's what it is. The way I look at it religion means being kind to others" (M50 El).
"Well, my idea is that you should do everything you can to help people and don't expect too much in return. You get looked down on though, if people think you're religious" (F40 Sec).

One person in seven made comments of this sort. Similar in implication, but different in angle of approach, were the replies of those who said religion meant having good principles, acting as one thought right, etc. The two groups merge, but in making the analysis an attempt was made to distinguish between those who looked on religion primarily as action, and those who looked on it as an attitude of mind producing action. On the borderline were those who made comments like:

"Well, I think living a fairly decent life. Not necessarily going to church, but if you're not doing any harm and trying to be decent in your own circle and leading a decent life it doesn't matter about going to church. Not so much, anyway" (F35 Sec).

This remark was classified in the first group, while the following just edges in to the second:

"Well, it's rather difficult to describe really. Actually, I should think different people have different views. I think it means a person leads a decent life and has got ideals and tries to live up to them. That's religion, I think" (F30 El).

Typical comments of those in the second group included:

"Well, I think it's to try not to do things against your conscience" (F19 Sec).

"Just a faith to keep people on the right roads of life" (M25 El).

"Well, to my mind it's the way you live. One's own principle. One does do something—or one doesn't do something" (M25 El).

"I think it's how their conscience guides them. The majority of people think what they do is right and I think it's a very great thing if you do what's right by yourself and other people" (F30 El).

An occasional comment showed more plainly the dissociation of the ethics of religion from people's ideas of the Churches:

"A philosophy of life to guide everyone, which in my opinion need not necessarily have anything to do with the Church. A philosophy of living by which we stand or fall" (M45 Sec).

But, on the other hand:

"Well I think it, apart from the actual reason, wanting to go to heaven, it makes you a better citizen—even if you don't believe in it. It makes you a good citizen. I don't go in for religious principles. I swear, smoke and drink, but when I go to church I forget all that" (M60 Sec).

It has been said that Christianity has become reduced to mere kindness, and there is some substance in the remark as applied to a good many people. But it confuses rather than illuminates the issue. Because, in our present culture, we have retained in a modified form some of the ethical principles and codes of behaviour associated with earlier systems and cultures, we do not say that the earlier system has "been reduced" to this small measure. All we say is that these principles remain acceptable, though the system as a whole has ceased to apply and to command belief. And this is very much what is happening to Christianity. Some of its principles are still acceptable and are often associated in people's minds with the religion from which they sprang. These remaining ethical principles, though cut off from their roots in faith and removed from their original context in a more complete code of behaviour, nevertheless remain basic in many lives. They are the nearer approach many people have to any static, sanctioned criterion for their everyday actions. And the trouble is not simply that they are in the nature of a hangover from the past, a debased form of Christianity, etc. The real trouble is that, out of context and out of pattern, these beliefs do not carry the conviction they did. We may well be witnessing the process of disintegration before rebuilding. The old surviving principles may be integrated into a new system, or there may be a revival of the old on modified lines. But there is a possibility, while the old system is disintegrating, that people may fall for some new seemingly all-embracing system of belief on tenuous grounds. The old beliefs began to disintegrate in the midst of a flood of new beliefs. But—and here we anticipate evidence which will be given later—many of the new beliefs have latterly begun to disintegrate too. We are not, to-day, witnessing the replacement of an old ethic by a virile new one, but the simple decay of a considerable number of guiding principles, replaced by no clear principle at all. The fact that some basic bits of Christian ethics still remain basic to so many people is perhaps the most definite sign for the future. Perhaps it is not entirely sentimental to suggest that the ordinary people of this country might refuse to countenance ideas which have found acceptance in places where the process of disintegration had gone further. The partial hangover of an ethic with which most people to-day are only partially acquainted is more steadying than no ethic. People who believe that religion means being kind, and that religion is a good thing, are at least fortified against some forms of indoctrination which a more complete lack of belief might admit.

Anti-Religion

When asked what they thought religion meant, about one man in five and one woman in eleven replied by criticising religion, religious people or the Church. Only a minority of comments, however, condemned religion as a whole. From young men particularly there were many remarks on these lines:

"Well, just a lot of tripe to me" (M16 El).

"Something I don't want to bother with" (M19 El).

"What you think about when you've nothing better to do" (M30 El).

"A lot of humbug" (M30 El).

"Oh, bothering about God and your soul" (F45 El).

"A lot of sobbing and praying and wasting of time" (F50 El).

Many dismiss religion thus as a matter of no interest, a waste of time. The most frequent comments, however, were those which criticised the behaviour of religious people. In fact, the first thing that comes into many people's minds when they hear the word "religion" is not the creed or dogma, but their conception of those who practise it. As one young man said:

"Well, what I think it means is hypocrisy through and through. I don't like religious people. I've got a grandmother like that. But it's old-fashioned, all that sort of thing" (M20 Sec).

Criticism of churchgoers was frequent in people's definition of religion:

"Going to church and being nasty about your neighbour if they don't see things the same way" (F25 Sec).

"A lot of bloody hypocrisy, if you ask me. Go to church and then tear your neighbour's character to tatters, that's all it is. There's worse people goes to church than stays at home. I can tell you that" (F30 El).

"People that think you can't lead a decent life without going to church and listening to the parsons and all that" (M25 El).

"Going off to church on Sundays and bowing and scraping to others that does the same" (M55 El).

"Oh, the parsons and the churchgoing and all the setting yourself up to be better than ordinary folk" (M45 Sec).

"Well, going to special places to kneel down and pray to what people think is God" (M18 El).

"Going to church and being preached at and singing some hymns and so on" (M25 El).

Some people defined religion as belonging to an exclusive sect, and there was a good deal of implicit and explicit criticism of the *motives* people are thought to have for practising religion:

"I associate it as an organised body having a particular dogma which is paraded as the genuine type of salvation" (M40 Sec).

"Well, it's a sect of people who believe their faith to be the only faith to save you after death" (M30 Sec).

"Taking care of what's going to happen to you when you're dead" (M70 El).

Others look on religion primarily as a money-making concern:

"Paying to keep the parsons" (M20 El).

"My opinion of religion is—nothing more than a monetary organisation" (M35 El).

"It's a money-making concern" (F30 El).

Remarkable by their comparative rarity were comments echoing the sentiment that religion is a narcotic, or a way of keeping people quiet:

"A means of fooling the much fooled working classes" (M35 Sec).

>"Something initiated to instal fear into the hearts of men and stop them from being heathen. Just a job" (M40 Sec).
>
>"Suffering evils gladly on the part of the poor and watching with a kind word and a condescending look on the part of the rich" (M40 El).

Considering the fact that so much of organised anti-religious propaganda in recent years has repeated sentiments of this sort, it is of some significance that these comments were so infrequent. People do not look on religion as something dangerous or calculated. For many it links up first in their minds with those they know who practise religious observances, or with organised religion and the Churches. But most criticism and ill-feeling is directed against *the people in religion* and not against religion itself.

So much for people's spontaneous definitions of religion. These comments show some of the factors which keep attention focused on a single aspect of the whole—ostentatious church-goers, formal practice unreflected in everyday actions and attitudes, the feeling that parsons make money out of their calling. They show that many people look on religion primarily as good acts, the beliefs inspiring these good acts being of secondary importance. But the attitudes we have described are only those which appear when people say what they *mean* by religion. They were also asked what their own attitude to religion was, and though this question only amplifies and confirms the results of the present one in some respects, it also brings out a number of new points of importance.

XI

ATTITUDES TO RELIGION

IN SAYING WHAT they meant by religion, there was a slight tendency for the more educated to define it in terms of belief and the less educated in terms of behaviour. The difference, however, was small and barely significant. When people were asked what was their attitude to religion, the replies of the more and less educated fell in practically identical proportions into the various groupings. As we have already shown, there is no important difference between these two groups in the extent to which they express belief in God. These numerical similarities obscure verbal differences, but they reveal an underlying sameness of attitude. Educated people who believe in God do tend to be more definite about it, but there are proportionately no more of them than less educated people. Those educated people who are associated at all with organised religion tend to be more closely associated with it than the less educated; but the proportions of each group who are *not* in any way associated with organised religion are similar. Identical proportions of more and less educated people say private prayers on occasion.

Generally speaking, it is true to say that such differences of attitude as do exist between those who left school at fourteen and those who had a lengthier education are chiefly ones of stress and coherence, not of basic belief. There are few signs in this material that current attitudes to religion are pronouncedly different between classes. We find the usual tendency for the less educated to be less able to express themselves or to give any opinion; and for the more educated to be more definite in the opinions they do give. But this is simply another way of saying that the less educated are less coherent in the use of words, and less able to follow through the implications of their thoughts. What we do not find with religion, and do find on many other subjects, is any major quantitative difference between the main lines along which more and less educated people are thinking.

Occupational details as well as details of education were collected in this survey, but a breakdown by occupation is likely to be misleading. It seemed particularly important in this investigation to isolate the effects of education as far as possible, and in order to do this the distribution of economic and occupational groupings had to be left to chance, except in so far as it was automatically determined by the sex, age and education stratification, and the method of sampling the area already described. The whole sample was composed as follows:

Professional and clerical	23 per cent.
Shop assistants and skilled working class	36 per cent.
Semi-skilled and unskilled	41 per cent.

This corresponds closely to the socio-economic stratification usually used by Mass-Observation, i.e. 20 per cent. upper and middle class, 40 per cent. artisan classes, 40 per cent. unskilled working class. Young and old were divided in almost identical proportions between the three main occupational groups. All married women were classified according to their husband's occupation, irrespective of whether they were working themselves or not. But the unmarried women had to be classified by their own occupation,[1] with the result that the women fell considerably more than the men into the semi-skilled and unskilled groups and into the clerical group. Because of this, any consideration of attitudes related to occupation has to be carefully examined to see whether differences are not in fact due to the different sex-composition of the different occupational grades.

The following apparent occupational differences were found on the basic question of belief in God:

Occupation	Percentage of the Following Group having this Occupation		
	Believers	Non-believers	Whole Sample
Professional, clerical	25	16	23
Shop, skilled	35	40	36
Semi-skilled, unskilled	40	44	41

[1] The usual socio-economic stratification used by Mass-Observation —"class" stratification—is itself partly an educational stratification, and was not suitable as a system of classification when education was also used.

On examination, however, the main difference here is found to be largely due to the predominance of women in the clerical jobs, and the preponderance of men in the skilled jobs. The apparent difference is mainly a reflection of sex differences in attitude, not occupational ones. It is probably true to say, however, that disbelief and agnosticism is most frequently found at the lowest economic and occupational levels, since here the occupational difference runs in the opposite direction to the sex difference (i.e. there is a preponderance of women, *and* a very slight preponderance of non-believers). If this is so, it is probably due to little more than the lesser ability of the lower occupational grades to form clear-cut attitudes rather than to any more positive disbelief. When allowance has been made for the different sex composition of the different occupational groups, we are left with little data that we did not know already from an examination of sex, age and education differences.

A breakdown of occupation by education shows:

Occupation	Percentage of the Following Group having this Occupation	
	Those with Elementary Education	Those with Secondary Education
Professional	1	35
Clerical	9	29
Shop and skilled	38	28
Semi-skilled	27	7
Unskilled	25	1

Thus education is itself a broad indication of occupational status. We cannot take the differences and similarities between more and less educated people as reflecting exactly the differences and similarities we should find between economic or occupational groups, but they are not likely to be far different.

For the reasons described, we have not used economic and occupational classifications in this report, but:

(*a*) Outstanding differences are reflected in the education classification.

(*b*) Other differences seem to be due rather to sex differences in the constitution of the various occupational groups than to actual differences between the occupational groups.

On most important points there are major differences between men and women, and between the generations; but class, however defined, appears to have little effect which is peculiar to this subject.

. . . . .

When people were asked what was their *own* attitude to religion, they replied as follows:

Attitude to Religion	Men	Women	Young	Old	Secondary Education	Elementary Education
Believe	20	24	13	31	18	23
Moderate approval	9	4	7	6	4	7
Church, formal observance, etc., necessary	3	9	6	6	9	5
Mention own sect only	10	17	12	15	14	14
	42	54	38	58	45	49
Don't believe	6	3	7	3	4	5
Anti-religious	10	3	7	6	9	6
Church, etc., not necessary	11	16	16	11	15	13
Not interested	19	12	19	12	16	15
	46	34	49	32	44	39
Other comments	4	1	1	4	2	3
Don't know	8	11	12	6	9	9

Here again is the familiar pattern, with men and young people markedly more critical than women and the old. In the above table an attempt is made on very broad lines to group together the favourable and unfavourable comments, but there is a great deal of overlap and ambiguity in this numerical presentation. A qualitative consideration of the results will show how attitudes are made up.

Tolerance—Apathy—Goodwill?

There was no very definite line of demarkation between those who are classified as showing moderate approval, and those classified as not interested. Some simply dismissed religion as outside their sphere of interest:

"I never bother about that sort of thing. It doesn't appeal" (M45 Sec).
"I'm sorry, but I've got no attitude towards religion" (M35 El).
"It doesn't interest me at all. I keep out of things like that—they're not in my line" (M20 Sec).
"I ignore it completely" (M30 Sec).
"I dunno, I've not got any attitude because I've not got any interest" (F35 El).

These dismissals merge into the comparatively rare comments of those who say they don't believe, culminating in the remark of a woman of thirty-five:

"I don't believe in nothing. I believe what is to be will be" (F35 El).

At the other end of the scale they merge into the comments of those who say that religion is harmless, all right for those who need it; and in general show that, though they personally aren't interested, they think there may be some use for it. Several younger people feel that religion is only suitable for the old:

"Doesn't touch me much—it's all right for women, especially when they're getting on a bit—but I don't think I need it just yet, thanks" (M30 El).
"Well, it's more for older people isn't it?" (M25 El).
"Ooh, I'm too young for religion" (M30 El).

Others say that religion is all right provided there is not too much of it:

"I think it's all right in a way, provided it's not overdone" (M40 El).
"Well, I don't know; it's all right in its place, I don't object to it altogether" (M18 El).

Or that anyone is entitled to believe what they like about it:

"Well, I let other people enjoy their beliefs. I haven't really any belief, but I'm tolerant of others" (F35 Sec).

"Well—er—if people want to do it, well, they can. I'm not stopping anyone. People who go to church three times a day don't know any more about it than those who go once a year. It's all right to a little extent" (F20 Sec).

"Well, I'm not biased in any shape or form. I'm 'live and let live.' I've not any set views" (M35 El).

"Well, as far as religion's concerned, if anyone wants to be religious, let them" (M30 El).

"It's all right for them as has time and inclination" (F50 El).

This broad and uninterested tolerance of religion is common —much more so than hostile feelings. Mass-Observation surveys at various times have shown some of the implications. Many people look upon religion as something quite harmless and purely personal—an innocuous hobby, like collecting stamps. One of the results of this attitude is that these same people often feel that religion is exceeding its legitimate grounds if it "interferes" with more practical matters. Religion to them is all right in its place, but it shouldn't get involved in everyday affairs outside the private life of believers.

In September, 1942, there was a meeting at the Albert Hall which provoked widespread interest at the time.[1] At this meeting the Archbishop of Canterbury made the statement that "the Church has not only a right, it has a duty, to declare the principles of true social life." Londoners were asked what they thought of this statement, and, if they showed signs of not understanding it, it was explained thus: "The Archbishop meant that the job of the Church was not only to do with religion, but just as much with everyday life."

While there was quite enthusiastic majority agreement with this sentiment a strong minority (33 per cent. of men, 15 per cent. of women) either disagreed or only half agreed. Some of this disagreement boiled down to little more than a general distrust of the Church and churchmen rather than with the

[1] Widespread interest for a religious gathering. Well over half of a London street sample did not know it had taken place.

sentiment expressed. But there was a very definite minority opinion that the Church would be exceeding its bounds if it announced the principles of true social life. Typical comments included:

"Everyone to his own job" (M50 El).

"They ought to stick to religion" (M60 El).

"I think the Church is the Church, don't you?" (F35 Sec).

"No, I don't agree with it. I think the Churches ought not to interfere with a thing like that" (M40 El).

"The Church is a purely spiritual thing. It shouldn't meddle with affairs of State" (M30 Sec).

"No. Keep out of it. There's a lot of trouble caused by religion. Like these wars" (F45 El).

It was significant that several of the half-critical remarks agreed with the word "duty," but challenged the word "right" in the Archbishop's statement. The idea of the Church, and of religion itself, as something which is and should be without power or rights in practical affairs, and should be concerned only with its duties towards the spiritual problems of individuals, is a frequent underlying one. Much of the existing goodwill towards religion among the non-religious is based on the idea that *religion is harmless*, and has little practical bearing on anything except the internal peace of mind of the religious. Positive goodwill borders on negative tolerance, and tolerance borders on apathy. A good deal, as we have shown, is nearer apathy. But the goodwill element must not be minimised. It is shown particularly clearly by people's attitudes to religious teaching in schools.

Religion in Schools

Two surveys have been made of people's opinions about the desirability of teaching religion in schools. The first, a questionnaire circulated to teachers in all types of school, showed that only one in ten of the teachers who replied were in favour of the entire exclusion of religious instruction from the school curriculum. Denominational instruction was a different matter, 70 per cent. of teachers thinking that it should not be provided in State-aided schools. But in all types of school a large majority favoured religious education of *some* sort.

The present sample were asked whether they thought religion should be taught in schools or not. Nearly everyone had an opinion on this question. Only one person in eight thought it should *not* be taught, less than one man in five, less than one woman in fourteen.

There was a remarkably close similarity between the views of men and women teachers and those of the ordinary men and women questioned:

> 21 per cent. of men teachers and 18 per cent. of the "ordinary" men favoured having no religious instruction in schools.
>
> 5 per cent. of women teachers and 7 per cent. of "ordinary" women favoured having no religious instruction in schools.

The difference between young and old was very slight on this question. While young people were less able to give an opinion and more inclined to say there should only be a little religious instruction, there was no difference in the proportion who thought there should be no such teaching at all.

Those with secondary education were slightly more inclined than those with elementary education to think that religion should not be taught, but the difference was not great. *Of the non-churchgoers, only 18 per cent. said it should not be taught; of the non-believers, only 27 per cent.*

If we examine the replies of those whose own personal religious beliefs are indefinite, confused or virtually non-existent, it is clear why so many of them favour religious instruction for children. They look upon it as the best way of imparting ethical principles—or, rather, they know of no alternative way of doing so. There was a wide range of spontaneous comment on these lines. All the following remarks were made by people who doubted or denied the existence of a Deity, said they never went to church, and did not believe in life after death:

> "There ought to be more religion in the younger generation. They're like a lot of heathens, stealing things from the

bombed houses. WE couldn't do that when I was a boy" (M35 El).

"Yes, I suppose it would teach the children to be kinder" (M18 El).

"Well, I don't know. Quite frankly, I think that perhaps they should, because it gives children an idea of what's right and wrong" (F30 El).

"Well, they say so, so's they shan't be barbarians. Well, I should think so—to make them civilised" (M65 El).

Very similar comments came from those whose own disbeliefs were less consistent. The following remarks were all made by people who said they believed in God:

"I certainly think some sort of religion should be taught to them. It's the only way to inspire a code of honour. Any is better than none, and it should be encouraged and some of this frivolity discouraged. People go their own way too much. I think you've got to have discipline" (M50 El).

"Everyone's happy in their own opinions. It doesn't matter which, does it? But children should be brought up on some foundation. You can't have them swearing all over the house and all that. You must have some means of control" (M50 El).

"Yes, definitely. It gives the children some backing, otherwise they'd be hard and selfish; they should be taught to think of others" (F45 El).

"If they learnt more about God there wouldn't be all these soldiers raping girls and doing girls in. A boy who's got God in his life would think twice" (F40 El).

"Yes—not too much. Sufficient to give them a belief and stop them from wandering into bad ways; that's all religion is for—something to believe in" (M25 El).

In these remarks we see the real basis of goodwill towards religion, even among those who have no religious beliefs themselves. The attitude of the old man, previously quoted, "It makes you a better citizen—even if you don't believe in it," succinctly expresses the underlying attitude of many others. Or, as another middle-aged man equally paradoxically said:

"Well, I'm very sorry I'm not religious, but I'm Christian. I'm very broadminded about religion, and I don't let them all have their own way. I'm very argumentative" (M55 El).

Thus, though very many people have discarded faith in the supernatural sanction behind the ethics of religion, they still look upon religion as the best way of inducing "good" behaviour: "sufficient to stop them wandering into bad ways, that's all religion is for." Another member of the older generation said that religion should be taught in school because "they won't teach them at home—won't even teach them to bath." And numerous comments made clear that the reason why many people believe in religious education is simply that they know of no other way in which elementary ethics can or will be taught. On this basis the sentiment "I'm not religious, but I'm Christian" makes sense, and makes it to many people. They would agree to the definition of the man who said religion is "whether you pay a regard to what you ought to do and don't just follow the guidance of your belly as you might say," and they would advocate religious instruction, not because they have a religious faith themselves, but because they still believe in the principles of conduct for which their own religious upbringing, however vague, is the only sanction they know. Because they know of no other effective sanction for conduct than the one they have rejected or cannot whole-heartedly accept. This complex structure of behaviour and attitude whose foundations are being eaten away rests very precariously on what remains of its original support. If it is considered that a minimal amount of religious instruction will provide an ethical grounding for life—and this, in less elaborate phraseology, is the frequent assumption —then it seems likely that people's ideas about religion will become still more confused, with the long-term result that the ethics imparted will become even more precariously based. Three Metrop clergymen, asked for their views on the current confusion in people's minds about religion, said:

1. "I think the cause of that is the Cooper-Temple clause

in the Education Act of 1870, which made the teaching of religion optional. We've now had two generations brought up without any definite religious teaching, and so nearly everyone below the age of sixty has woolly ideas about it—the non-churchgoing part of the community, that is. I think that is one of the biggest stumbling-blocks we have to deal with. . . . And *why* do they leave off going to Sunday School at fourteen? Because their parents don't go to church. They all tell you they don't go themselves, 'but I always see the children go to Sunday school.' . . . Then I ask why they've stopped going. 'Oh, he's fourteen now,' just as if that explained everything. Naturally enough, when they're old enough, they copy their parents, who don't go to church. And the fact they don't go after they reach the age of fourteen also explains their woolly ideas" (Church of England Vicar).

2. "I think the majority of people have an entirely materialistic attitude—they take the wrong thing for religion—they come to church when it's a question of being married or buried or baptised, but that's all. The whole mischief lies in the want of religious education in the schools—we shall never get right until each denomination gives religious instruction to its own children. Thirty or forty years ago we were up against a generation of parents who used to go to church as children, ceased to go, but liked their children to go. Now we're up against a generation of *parents* who never went . . ." (Anglo-Catholic Vicar).

3. "There's no doubt that the majority of people don't know what the Christian faith is. Much of it is just memories of childhood teaching. And you can't teach children as you can grown people—you tell them Bible stories and so on, and that probably accounts for the confusion in their minds now—they've never faced up to it as adults . . ." (Church of England Vicar).

A reflection of the goodwill hangover is the remark of a non-churchgoing mother who said: "Oh, yes, I think it's nice for children to be taught to believe in Christ. I *do* think it's nice." In the light of the material we have discussed, we can transcribe this sentiment. People feel it's nice for their children to be taught to be good, in the sense they understand Christianity means by being good—that is, chiefly, to be kind and considerate of other people. It's nice to be nice. Slighter ethical principles can be imagined than this. But, so long as the ultimate sanction for being nice and kind is such a flimsy one, it is likely that even this principle may weaken under slight pressure of alternative.

Whatever one's views on religion, the fact that so much of to-day's routine behaviour is founded on Christian teaching is of primary importance. For the Christian, the moral will be to strengthen and broaden the principles through faith and understanding. For the non-Christian there are many possible morals, but each involves *either* incorporating the ethical remnants in a more cohesive, understood, interest-provoking whole—*or* providing a new ethic which is a worthy successor to the old. Neither side can neglect the position implicit in the existence of a loosely and superficially believed-in code for conduct, if they accept the proposition put forward at the beginning of this book. People are not happy without accepted standards and criteria for their actions; in proportion as they find the old standards weakening within them and without, they look round the more eagerly for new. Aldous Huxley's recent comment is *apropos*, though agreement with his facts is not acceptance of his implications:

> "To the surprise of the Humanists and Liberal Churchmen, the abolition of God left a perceptible void. But Nature abhors vacuums. Nation, Class and Party, Culture and Art have rushed in to fill the empty niche. For politicians, and for those of us who happen to have been born with a talent, the new pseudo-religions have been, still are and (until they destroy the entire social structure) will continue to be extremely profitable superstitions."

There is no need to believe that all replacements for religion must be pseudo-religious superstitions in order to agree that the nature of the vacuum-filler is, under present conditions, largely a matter of chance.

XII

TIME, RITUAL AND ETHICS

"Life's too fast for people to be interested. At one time when travel and entertainment were next to impossible for the majorities it gave them an interest. To-day it palls."

THUS A MIDDLE-CLASS woman of thirty-five. And a young factory worker of nineteen:

"It was all right when I was young. I didn't understand any different. As you get older you find other things—learn of things that take up your time, especially at week-ends, when you like to go out. In my opinion, it's a waste of time, but if you feel that going to Sunday school or church makes you better—go. I think quite a lot of it's a farce, because you hear someone tell you they know or heard of some incident where preachers have just been money-grabbers. Seventy-five per cent. of them are all right, I suppose."

Time and opportunity are at a premium in this generation. Paradoxically, in an epoch when working hours are shortening, the State providing more and more of the services which previously involved the individual in time-spending, and labour-saving time-saving devices (from the cheap restaurant to the vacuum-cleaner) are reducing steadily the hours which must be spent on life's chores, the time element seems a greater obstacle than ever. Of their attitude to religion, people said:

"Well, I think you should live your own life the best you can. If I'd time to go I should like to go. As it is I try to live my own life the best I can" (F35 El).

"I've got no time. I believe in it, but I've got no time" (F30 El).

"It's all right for folks as need it—but I work too hard. God won't feed my children" (F35 El).

It is partly this sense of multitudinous things to do which is at the back of people's impatience with the paraphernalia of religion—churchgoing, ritual, kneeling down to pray. At the same time, there is the feeling that they are just as well qualified to work out their religion on their own as to take it on authority, or to adhere to set forms:

"I can't be bothered with it. There are so many interesting things to be done, and you must admit the Church doesn't move with the times" (F20 El).

"Well, I believe in the Almighty Being and I believe in the Hereafter, but I mind my own opinions and I don't bother about the parsons and the archbishops. When I see an archbishop gets £10,000 a year, I think he's only in it for the money and I know as much about the Almighty as he does" (M60 El).

"I don't bind myself to a particular sect. I say lead a decent life and help lame dogs over stiles. Help others and help yourself without detriment to other people. My leanings are towards Nonconformists. They don't read their prayers out of books, and I always think if you pray it should come from the heart" (M50 Sec).

"I don't know what you mean by religion. We must believe in God above or we wouldn't be here ourselves. You can be good at home" (F55 El).

"I've not got the time, and I think if you can't be good in your own home you won't get any better by going to church. I say my prayers and all that, and I had baby christened, but I've not got a lot of use for churchy people" (F25 Sec).

Add to this the more positive anti-Church feelings already discussed, and we have a large body of people whose religion is *ostensibly* something they have "worked out for themselves," and which they have no intention of checking on orthodoxy. Consider, then, the fact that most people think religion should be taught in schools—an ostensibly inconsistent attitude among the clear majority of non-believers who express it, but one which we have explained as showing that many people look upon religion as the only way of teaching their children *principles* of behaviour. In their comments, several people, though thinking religion should be taught, showed anxiety that the children should not be indoctrinated:

"Children have to be taught to be good, and it's one way of doing it. But not too much. Not all this fear of God" (F35 Sec: non-believer).

"Well, half an hour a week we used to learn. Once or twice a week is all they need. It's no use though if they just pack it up" (F20 Sec: believer).

"Not crammed. To a certain extent. It keeps them within bonds. But there's other things more essential" (M70 Sec: non-believer).

"Yes, but it ought to be explained—not taught as though it was infallible" (M35 Sec).

Others were afraid that religious education would stop children "thinking for themselves."

"Yes, but not on any strict line—C. of E. or R.C. or Nonconformist—they should be taught about the Gospels, and then they can learn the rest for themselves freely when they're of age" (F50 Sec: believer).

"I don't know. Children haven't much alternative if they're taught it young. Teach them the elements and let them carry on afterwards if they want to" (M30 Sec: believer).

"I think religion should be for later years. I had it from five onwards, and we couldn't think for ourselves" (M25 Sec: non-believer).

And, at the extreme:

"If religion is taught in schools it will produce automatons with no capacity for independent thought—they'll have the herd mind. I wouldn't like to see it taught in schools" (M40 Sec).

There were also several spontaneous suggestions that more than one religion should be taught:

> "Yes, but all the religions should be put before them, not just the one—Christianity" (F30 Sec).
>
> "I don't think they should be made to follow any set religion. They should have a choice" (M20 Sec).
>
> "I don't believe children should be biased and taught just one religion, but general principle religions, and let them choose for themselves when they're better able to understand" (F25 El).

Though each single type of comment was not frequent, the total number of people who considered, in one way or another, that religious education should be informative and not didactic was considerable. The complementary side of the picture is given by the remarks of those who, looking for some means of expressing their conception of religion, were unable to find any other way of explaining it than "what I learnt at school" or "what I was brought up to believe":

> "I'd say religion is a certain belief to which you're born into, all according to what your parents are" (F40 El).
>
> "It's sort of what you're taught to believe, and I do believe in what I'm taught. I can't see any other way for the world to exist otherwise. It's believing in something you've never seen" (F20 El).
>
> "I think it's what you're taught in Sunday school. If you're C. of E., you believe in that, and if you're Catholic, you believe in that—there's all sorts" (F30 El).

And, at a more intellectual level:

> "Well, I don't know what the literal translation is. Belief founded upon . . . what can I say now . . . handing down of a sort of . . . well, what can you say . . . rather difficult . . . religion . . . strike me . . . what you're taught to believe as youngsters . . . handed down from generation to generation. You can grow out of it. It's my view you can" (M40 Sec).

The fear that religious education will stop children thinking for themselves was expressed mainly by the more educated people, and its conscious importance at other levels must not be overstressed. But there does seem to be a fairly common confusion of attitude, in that people definitely want the rudiments of ethics taught on a religious basis, but equally definitely don't want the religious side of the education to produce too strong or dogmatic a faith. The teacher who tries to fit his instruction into this pattern is faced with the alternative of either becoming chiefly an exponent of rational ethics and leaving the supernatural in the background; or of hedging the supernatural round with so many qualifications that the divinely inspired ethics are likely to command an equally qualified acceptance. And the dilemma is not confined to teachers. It is not easy for parents to teach their children "the difference between right and wrong" if their basis for acknowledging the difference is a divine revelation in which they only half-heartedly believe. If children are to be left open-minded about God, God is a poor basis on which to attempt to build up a code of behaviour.

In the above-mentioned postal enquiry among schoolteachers, when teachers were asked if they thought that, if an agreed syllabus were adopted, it should include instruction in the chief faiths of the world, 61 per cent. replied in the affirmative. In the present enquiry, ordinary men and women were asked if they knew anything about any other religion besides Christianity and Judaism: 86 per cent. of the whole sample (94 per cent. of women, and 91 per cent. of those with elementary education) said they didn't; and a considerable proportion of those who said they did had only a vague inkling of ritual picked up from films or fiction reading.[1]

[1] Mohammedanism and Buddhism are the most known-about religions—about one person in ten claims to know something about them. About one in thirty-five say they know something about Hinduism, and the same proportion say they know something about Confucianism. But note that the vaguest inaccurate smattering counts as knowledge in a prestige question of this sort. Several of the 14 per cent. who say they know something about another religion mention "paganism," which covers a multitude of things, some the invention of fiction writers. The number of people who claimed to know anything was so small that it did not seem worth putting them through a test of knowledge. Had we done so, it is quite clear that many would have failed to pass it.

Considering all the facts outlined in this report so far, we may summarise the situation thus:

1. Here we have a community, the majority of whose members have at most a slight knowledge about any sort of religious doctrine. The majority think there is, or probably is, a God of some sort. A good many think there may well not be, and a not insignificant minority think there isn't.

2. Belief or non-belief is becoming more and more a purely private affair. Belief is becoming less and less associated with any recognised religious system, and believers correspondingly less acquainted with religious dogma or the outline of religious ethics. Ostensibly many people's religion to-day is one they have "worked out for themselves." In fact, this means in most cases that it is based on a narrower acquaintance with its sources than before. It is not a new religion, but an incomplete version of the old, commanding less faith, covering a less wide field.

3. There is a common basic code of behaviour accepted by most members of this community, and they are "shocked" when they see people deviating from it. When they are asked what they mean by religion, many of them answer in terms of this code of behaviour. And this includes many whose faith in the existence of a Deity is very shaky indeed, or even non-existent.

4. Though the same code of behaviour could be based on something other than religion, such as a rational ethic, in point of fact it isn't—and this fact is tacitly acknowledged when "non-religious" people say religion "means" what they consider good actions; and when they say that their children should be taught religion so that they will "know right from wrong."

5. We thus have a code which people *feel* is based on religious teachings, but to which they adhere without knowing much about these teachings, and without having much faith in the validity of their ultimate sanction. In so far as many people's code of behaviour is still religion-based, they are in the position of saying: "I think this is a good way to behave; but I'm not really convinced that my reasons for thinking so are valid."

6. Some of the problems which present themselves are these: To what extent is this code of behaviour likely to persist if

religious faith continues to weaken? Assuming there are desirable elements in it, to what extent will they continue, so to speak, on their own momentum? To what extent would a more positive breakdown in religion mean a breakdown in ethics? What, if anything, offers itself to-day in place of the ethics of religion, and to what extent does it appear to be commanding acceptance? Knowing, as we do, that even among those who believe in God, there are many who believe there is nothing to follow life on this earth, to what extent are related ideas affected by this concentration on earthly life? And, spiritual values being relegated to a very secondary place in most people's lives, how is that affecting their outlook?

XIII

PURPOSE OF LIFE

PEOPLE WERE ASKED whether they had any ideas about the purpose of life on this earth. If they said no, or couldn't reply, they were asked informally: "Well, what do you think we're here for?" If they were still unable to reply, they were asked if they'd ever thought about it at all. On this basis, 20 per cent. said they'd never thought about it, while another 17 per cent. said they didn't know. Clearly, this figure means little on its own, but it is of some interest to compare it with the corresponding figure for two other questions we shall discuss shortly. These two questions concerned what people thought the most important thing in life, and what they thought the way to get the best from life:

    37 per cent. were unable to give any ideas about the purpose of life.

    17 per cent. were unable to say what they thought the most important thing in life.

    15 per cent. were unable to say what they thought the way of getting the best from life.

People are, rather naturally, much more ready with a pat, immediate answer on how to live life than they are to suggest why life is being lived at all.

The present question was not, of course, intended to go at all deep into people's attitudes. But verbal responses at the superficial level of an interview have their special meaning and implications. This verbal level is the one with which the priest, the reformer, the idealist, the politician is first confronted when he attempts to influence a crowd of people in the direction of his beliefs. Later he may discover the underlying roots of these verbal attitudes, and he will exercise a greater influence by attacking the root than by indulging in a prolonged argumentative squabble with the verbal symptoms. But it is the symptoms which at the same time give a clue to the cause and render it more difficult of access. Over years of attitude formation people build up a verbal barrier against their deeper feelings. To-day's barrier is cynicism and scepticism, and it is part of the intention of this report to describe the barrier in the words of ordinary men and women from which it is made up. But in doing so we must not lose sight of the fact that we *are* describing symptoms and not the underlying condition from which they arise. Such a description is a necessary preliminary to diagnosis; it is not diagnosis itself.

Moreover, the study of answers to this question is further complicated by the ambiguity of the question, which could not have been cleared up without something like a Socratic development of the answers—and this, of course, was far beyond the scope of the interviews. Thus it is clear that the answers as they stand are replies to one or more of at least four different questions, viz.: (1) What, do you think, is the purpose of God for human beings in the world? (2) What ought our purpose in life to be? (3) What is your purpose in life? (4) What is the good of life?

Sometimes it is clear, sometimes it is not clear, to which of these questions a reply is being given. However, it seems on the whole fair to assume that those who expressed doubt about the purpose of life were expressing doubt about the value of life; were, for the most part, people who had no firm conception of life's good, and no strong purpose in their own lives. This assumption should be qualified by the recognition that the reflective person who has rejected belief in God will understand and answer this question in the first sense, and will therefore appear doubtful or negative about the purpose of life, although he may have firm purposes and ideals of his own.

Bearing these considerations in mind, the replies of the 63 per cent. who were able to say something about the purpose of life may be roughly divided into:

(*a*) those which suggest that the person making them accepts the idea that life is directed towards some purpose,

(*b*) those which suggest that the person is doubtful whether life is directed to a purpose.

Results were:

Purpose of Life	Percentage saying Life is for this Purpose
Group (a): Doing Good	18 ⎱ 24
Making a better world	6 ⎰
Preparation for the next life	5
Happiness, happy home life	4
Righteousness, being good	3
Pleasure	2
Total, Group (a),	38 per cent.
Group (b): Procreation	7
To fulfil a purpose unknown	7
Work	6
No purpose	5
Cynical	1
Total, Group (b),	26 per cent.

Eight per cent. made other miscellaneous comments and several people made comments falling into more than one category, so that the percentages add to over 63 per cent. But the double comments mostly fell into Group (a). Roughly speaking, among the two-thirds who are able to say anything about the purpose of life, there are five whose comments suggest doubt as to whether life has a purpose for every seven whose comments suggest that it *has*.

Purpose

The commonest answer of all was that the "purpose of life is to do good to others":

"Well, just to try and do good and kindness to all people and there'll never be any hatred or anything" (F20 El).

"Just goodwill and things like that. Being friendly to your neighbour like you read about. I'd do anyone a good turn within my power, you know" (M30 El).

"Well, I meself think the purpose of life is to look after yourself and study other people according to your ability and try to love everybody as far as you can. Love your neighbour, in fact. But I don't class Germans as your neighbour, not under the present régime" (M60 El).

"Well, it's to do good to others. Help others and not think of yourself too much. The world's too selfish" (M65 Sec).

"I think we're here to do the best for one another, but I don't know what purpose" (F30 Sec).

This type of reply was given with equal frequency by believers and non-believers in God.

Those who said we were here to make the world a better place:

"Don't you think that we're put on earth in order that each generation may contribute its share. We've got to help build the world" (M50 El).

"To discharge your duty and leave the place a better place in so far as you're able" (M35 El).

"I should imagine you've got to work to build a home and all that sort of thing and do your job as well as you're able so that others coming after you can benefit" (M25 El).

The 5 per cent. who said we were here to prepare for the next life were naturally all believers, as were nearly all of those who said we were here to be good or righteous. On the other hand twice as many non-believers as believers said we were here for pleasure or happiness.

No Purpose?

The comments in the second group, given by about one person in four (and a considerably higher proportion of those able to express any ideas at all on the subject), nearly all boil down to the sentiment of the old song: "We're here because we're here because we're here because we're here." Seven per cent. said, in effect, that the purpose of life is that life shall continue:

"Insects, ants, you wonder what they've got as a purpose. Production. Same as plant life. They grow. Seeds blow, and all that" (M55 Sec).

"Well, it's hard to say. I expect it's to make the numbers up, and when there's too many of us we get killed off, same as insects. That's where wars come in" (F50 El).

"Work, eat, sleep, goodness knows what. Make the generations, I suppose" (F30 El).

"I always think to keep the generations going. The populations" (F30 El).

"The main purpose is reproduction. We're here for that, really" (M20 Sec).

A similar proportion said, in effect, that the purpose of life was to fulfil the purpose of life. Why this type of comment was classified here is illustrated by an example from a young man:

"Well, I think we're all cogs of one big machine, but what I'm wondering is: What is the machine for? That's your query" (M20 El).

Though one or two individuals who took this attitude seemed to feel that the nameless purpose was a good one, the following were more typical:

"We're here to do just a certain amount, and carry on in whatever state of life you start in. It's mapped out for you. You can't get out of it whatever you try. If you're born to be lucky, it don't matter" (M70 Sec).

"We must be here for a purpose—the world wouldn't go on if we weren't here—that's what I can't help thinking must be our purpose" (F45 El).

"I don't think we're here for any particular motive, but that we're here to make up a whole. A composite part of Nature, as I've already said" (M40 Sec).

The first of these examples is reminiscent of the attitude of the woman who, asked whether she believed in God, said she did, definitely, and gave as her reason: "You intend to do wrong and there's something comes up and baulks you at every turn you take."

Then there were those who said that the purpose of life was to work. Most of them said, in effect, that the purpose of life was to keep alive, and with them may be grouped the small number of miscellaneous cynical comments:

"Oh, to get the money to get your food, that seems to be all the purpose there is" (F18 El).

"Earn some money, have a good life, and then drop dead and go back where we came from" (F25 El).

"All I can see is work. Work to live. If you don't work you don't live" (M60 El).

"To work hard to keep the blokes at the top fat and well fed" (M30 El).

To which must be added the remark of the old man of seventy-five who said that the purpose of life was to die:

"From what I can see it's get off as quick as you can and make room for someone else. There's not really much to live for" (M75 El).

And, finally, there was the group who said that they didn't think life had a purpose at all:

"Well . . . you . . . that's just the point. If you believe in a Deity, you believe in a purpose. If you think this world is doing well, have another look round. If this chaos to-day is part of a divine plan, I give up" (M60 Sec).

"I've been studying my fellow men and women for the past forty years, and the more I look at them, the more I wonder myself why they're here" (M60 El).

"I don't think we're here for any special purpose except to fill up the place" (M18 El).

There were some borderline cases which verged on saying there was no purpose, but were sometimes given the benefit of the doubt:

"Don't know that life ever struck me as having a purpose. Except to work and enjoy yourself and better yourself if you can" (M25 El).

"I should imagine we're just here to live. After all, what are the birds here for?" (M25 El).

"Now you've caught me. I've no idea. My life's all work and having babies" (F40 Sec).

Of all the comments in Group (*b*), the most unambiguously doubtful-of-purpose are those in the categories Procreation, Work, No Purpose and Cynical. This type of comment was made by over twice as many non-believers as believers, and this despite the fact that the non-believers were rather less able than the believers to say anything definite in answer to the question. Of those who doubt the existence of God, or disbelieve in it, one in three made a remark of this kind about the purpose of life. The extent to which this is a result of non-believers understanding the question in the first of the four senses (mentioned on p. 99) may be judged from the comments already quoted.

The non-believers whose comments come in Group (a) say very much the same things as the believers. There is, for instance, no tendency for non-believers to say more often than believers that the purpose of life is to build a better world. The conclusions to be drawn are mainly negative. There are no signs here that those who have given up supernatural beliefs are finding satisfying human purpose in life; only that they are more doubtful whether it has value at all. When they think it has a value, their replies are practically the same as those of believers. Do they think the same thing for a new reason, or for less reason? And is their doubt about life's general purpose replaced by a new sense of individual purpose? There are some indications in the following discussion.

XIV

THE MOST IMPORTANT THING

WHEN PEOPLE WERE ASKED what they thought the most important thing in life, their replies covered so wide a range that any numerical analysis is of interest chiefly in showing the differences between groups rather than giving any clear indication of the nature of replies. The following list shows, in order of frequency with which they were mentioned, roughly the sort of things which people say are most important:

1. Happiness, happy home life.
2. Health.
3. Family.
4. *Doing* good.
5. Money.
6. Love, marriage.
7. Righteousness, *being* good.
8. Pleasure, having a good time.
9. Living, life, getting the best out of things.
10. Work.
11. Faith.

In this analysis a very wide variety of comments come into some categories. "Love and marriage," for instance, ranges from the remark of a young man who said the most important thing was "Falling in love with a beautiful woman," to that of the girl who replied: "I should say to earn your bread or else get married." In several other categories there is an equally tenuous link between the implications at one end of the series and the other.

Group differences, though mostly slight between single categories, become considerable when related categories are taken together. Though women were less able to answer the question than men, they mention love, marriage and the family twice as often; whereas men mention health and money twice as often as women. All those who said that faith was the most important thing were women (one in twenty of them). Men said that happiness and pleasure were the most important things in life much more often than women. In the light of verbatim comments, we can interpret these differences as showing the different focus of the two sexes—men being chiefly concerned with earning a living, keeping fit to do it, and relaxing after it; women with getting a husband, raising a family, and making a success of it.

Young and old people were about equally able to answer the question, but old people said doing good was the most important thing three times as often as young. They mentioned health twice as often. Young people said that love or marriage was the most important thing much more often than old. A quarter of the younger generation mentioned happiness and pleasure, compared with only one in seven of older people.

The difference between more and less educated people was slight. The more educated were less inclined to think health of paramount importance—but this simply implies that, with their higher living standards, and greater economic security, health problems do not loom so large in their lives. More important is the fact that those with secondary education say the family is the most important thing less often than any other group. Only 4 per cent. mention it, compared with 13 per cent. of those with elementary education.

Non-believers were much less inclined than believers to say that doing good, or being good was the most important thing (7 per cent. to 20 per cent.); and rather more inclined to say that pleasure and happiness were the most important things (26 per cent. to 18 per cent.). All those mentioning independence were non-believers (one in twenty-five of them).

As we have said, the replies grouped in each of the categories used are by no means homogeneous. We can, however, take some groups as representing what might broadly be called an "interdependent" outlook, and some as representing an "independent" outlook. Love, marriage, the family, doing good, righteousness, faith, all imply some sort of dependence on others. Pleasure, money, independence, do not. Happiness, though the replies thus classified are more of the interdependent than the independent type, is not entirely one thing or the other, and is best left out of this re-grouping. Other categories omitted from consideration are also shown by the verbatims to be of an ambiguous nature.[1]

If we break down these groups of attitude by the religious beliefs of those expressing them, we find:

Most Important Thing In Life	Percentage saying this is the Most Important Thing among—				
	Non-believers	Whole Sample	Believers	Church of England Churchgoers	Roman Catholic Churchgoers
"Interdependent" things	22	38	43	40	53
"Independent" things	22	15	12	9	7

Thus, the proportion of people who take what we have called an "independent" line when asked what they consider the most important thing in life declines as religious belief and discipline strengthens. A similar breakdown for sex, age and education groups shows:

Most Important Thing in Life	Percentage saying this is the Most Important Thing among				
	Men	Women	Young	Old	Secondary Education	Elementary Education
"Interdependent" things	29	47	32	43	38	37
"Independent" things	21	9	18	13	14	15

There is thus, on these broad lines, no difference between the attitudes of more and less educated people. It is characteristic of the findings of this survey that often educational factors have only a small effect on the attitudes under consideration. There are differences in detail, and considerable differences in form of expression, but on points of major significance there is usually little or none.

The young are less inclined than the old to give the "interdependent" replies, but the difference in the proportion giving "independent" answers is slight. The main difference is that between the sexes, with men much more inclined to give

[1] What we have called "interdependence" and "independence" must not be confused with selfishness and unselfishness. The verbatim comments show that this would be a serious misrepresentation of the facts.

"independent" replies, and much less inclined to give "interdependent" ones.

"Independent" purpose, in this sense, is thus concentrated among non-believers, among men, and probably to a slight extent among the young. Thus expressed, there is no indication whether active individualism, passive isolationism, or something else is implied. The best way of assessing the implications is to run through the replies of the 120-odd men under forty, and pick out all those who are non-believers and who made comments of the kind we have called "independent" (pleasure, money, independence). Here they are, at random:

"Having a good time."

"Money."

"Well, it's hard to say, but it's no pleasure to you if it's not worth the living of it."

"Swimming for me, always."

"Myself."

"Well, doing the best for yourself."

"Enjoying yourself."

"Money—all I can see of it."

"I should think it's life itself."

"Well, to enjoy it, I should say."

"To be able to live your own life."

"For me, to be a musician."

"At present to get as much fun out of life as I can."

"Just to keep on living."

"Money—without it we can do nothing."

"Well, I think the most important thing is not to let other folks lead you by the nose—to keep yourself well and fit and see that you get a real kick out of life."

"Money."

"Improving one's culture."

"Making the best of things. Having a good time while you're here."

"Well, to get all the pleasure you can without hurting anyone else."

Before commenting further, let us examine the results of a related question. People were asked what they thought was the way of getting the best from life. They replied as follows:

Way of getting the Best from Life	Percentage saying this is the Way of getting the Best from Life
Doing Good	25
Take it as it comes, happiness, contentment	14
Righteousness, being good	13
Pleasure	8
Work	8
Independence	7
Money	6
Family	4
Living, etc.	2
Moderation	1
Faith	1
Other comments	16
Don't know	15

The group differences were similar in this question to the previous one. Again extracting the three "independent" groups of comment—pleasure, money, independence—we may compare results for the two questions:

Group	Percentage among this group saying Pleasure, Money or Independence were: (a) the most important thing in life; (b) the way of getting the best from life	
	(a)	(b)
Men	21	31
Women	9	10
Young	18	26
Old	13	14
Secondary education	14	20
Elementary education	15	21
Non-believers	22	24
Believers	12	19
Church of England churchgoers	9	17
Roman Catholic churchgoers	7	12

In the second question there is an increase in the extent to which men and young people give the "independent" replies, but no change in the proportion of women and old people who give them. The two questions may be considered as complementary, the second tending to draw out from people those aspects of importance-to-living not mentioned in their replies to the first. It is clear that men, young people, non-believers are the ones who predominantly take the "independent" outlook. Let us again pick out at random the replies of young male non-believers who give "independent" replies on the way of getting the best from life. In the following examples, their answer to the question on the purpose of life is given first (P); then what they say is the most important thing in life (I); and, finally, their way to get the best from life (B):

1. P. "I should imagine we're just here to live. After all, what are birds here for?"
   I. "Falling in love with lovely women; there's nothing more important."
   B. "Enjoying yourself, to do what you want to do if you consider it's good for you."

2. P. "To keep your health and have a good time."
   I. "Well, doing the best for yourself."
   B. "Well, to go out and get what you want I should say. Make up your mind what you want and then get it. I don't believe in just grumbling because things are what they are. I believe in getting a good time, anyway."

3. P. "Well, to have kids to carry on the country."
   I. "Enjoying yourself."
   B. "Well, to look out for enjoyment and not be mopey."

4. P. "All hard work and not much fun, is it?"
   I. "Money—all I can see of it."
   B. "Work as hard as you can. Get some of this [waving ten-shilling note] and have a good time, I suppose."

5. P. "Well, I believe in the present day, every person for himself. Don't ask the other fellow for it. The saying is, me and Jack's at work, I can't give him anything. And if another fellow's got anything, he won't give me £1."

    I. "I should think it's life itself."
    B. "Anything you like to go for."

6. P. "God only knows."
    I. "Got me beat again."
    B. "Go out and enjoy yourself."

7. P. "Just to have as good a time as you can without acting mean to anyone else."
    I. "Well, to enjoy it, I should say."
    B. "Dunno. Go out and enjoy yourself. Don't mope around."

8. P. "Well, I suppose it's to do as your fathers and grandfathers did; get married and have a home and kids and provide for them. I should think that's the idea."
    I. "Well, it's hard to say, but it's no pleasure to you if it's not worth the living of it."
    B. "Why, to enjoy it. Not to have a miserable outlook on it."

9. P. "Well, to have a good time; make the best of it."
    I. "I dunno. Never thought about it."
    B. "Well, make up your mind to enjoy yourself, and never mind what happens."

10. P. "Just to work and earn money and go to bed and sleep."
    I. "Swimming for me always."
    B. "Enjoying it while you can."

11. P. "That I can't tell."
    I. "Can't tell you."
    B. "Well, that's another thing. Just do what you like and let no one interfere with you. Nowadays you can't, though."

12. P. "We haven't one, apart from the parts we play in ordinary life."
    I. "Myself."
    B. "Taking care of myself."

13. P. "Purpose? I've got a rough idea, but . . ."
    I. "I don't really know how to answer that."
    B. "Well, do what you want to do yourself. Be free and easy. Don't give a damn for anyone."

14. P. "Don't know—to work."
    I. "When you retire, I suppose."
    B. "Have as much fun as you can."

The association between this sort of attitude and lack of religious beliefs may well be put down to the predominance of women and old people among the religious, and it may be objected that these have always been the attitudes of youth and of the male sex: the fact that these same groups are the ones which are losing religious faith is coincidental. Certainly, we cannot say that their lack of religious beliefs is *causing* people to have these attitudes, nor that the attitudes are *causing* them to lose faith. There is no sign, however, that the non-religious are adopting a more "interdependent," cooperative attitude than the religious. The signs point the other way, and, in so far as the decay of religious beliefs is releasing energy into new channels, the energy is being released chiefly into hedonistic and individualistic ones.

We have given examples of these attitudes among the young. Older people who gave the "independent" replies usually adopted a rather different tone:

"To enjoy yourself and don't worry too much about the future. Chances are you won't be there to see it" (M45 Sec).

"Mind my own business. I keep my mouth shut" (M65 El).

"Oh, make your own amusements. Take no notice of anyone else. Make up your own" (M60 El).

"Hold your tongue and be careful what you tells people" (M55 El).

"Don't interfere with anyone else's life and you'll find life's not so bad" (M45 El).

"To lead your own life and mind your own business and look after yourself. I don't believe in looking after others—they don't trouble about you" (F45 El).

Interdependent

Of the "interdependent" attitudes, the most frequent was "Being kind," and the form it most usually took was: "Do as you would be done by," "To treat others as you want to be treated," etc. The Golden Rule was expressed in many ways, though only once in an approximation to the words of Christ (and Kipling?): "Well now, I should say carry on and play the game. Do unto others as you want them to do unto you" (M50 Sec). Several people made it clear that they thought do-as-you-would-be-done-by promised good returns and made for personal popularity:

> "If you're helpful to others, they generally reciprocate" (M50 El).
>
> "Be nice to other people and others in return will be nice to you" (M20 El).
>
> "Well, if you're kind and give to others you get repaid back. Have a nice nature and always do good turns, you get happiness back. Otherwise you're not much liked" (F30 El).

Compare also "cast thy bread upon the waters . . ." which ranged from:

> "Put as much into it as possible and you'll get most out of it" (M30 Sec).

to:

> "Give what you can to other people—you'll get it back in the long run" (M25 El).

And the safety-first principle:

> "I think the best way is to treat everyone as they treat you" (M40 El).

But many of those who preferred the kind, helpful, generous way of getting the best from life, were clearly not thinking of such immediate reciprocation:

> "Well, I don't know. I know I get a lot of fun out of doing things for other people and giving things to them" (F25 Sec).

"Well, I always find if you help anyone you're getting the best out of life by making someone happy. You feel you've done something for someone" (F35 El).

"To do somebody else a good turn and not look for any reward" (F30 El).

"By being honest and straightforward and, if you can, do a good turn to them. It doesn't mean that if you support charity that that's your good deed. There's a woman over the road, for instance. She's nothing to me, but she went to hospital with an illegitimate child and no one would take her in, so we did. That's a good turn" (M45 El).

It is because each group of attitudes is made up of such a mixture of altruism and near-opportunism that we indicated earlier that any suggestion of a distinction between selfishness and unselfishness would be misleading. What we can see clearly is a distinction between those who spontaneously look upon their fulfilment in life as dependent on their relation with others, and those who look upon it as dependent on what they can do for themselves. It is the dependent-on-self fulfilments which are associated with lack of religious beliefs, and which are on the up-grade to-day.

Golden Rule—Golden Mean

Though few people actually advocated moderation *per se* as the way to get the best from life, the idea of moderation is a very frequent theme. Here are examples in which this typical moderation note is struck:

"I believe in making the best of things. I'm one of those persons who don't believe in extremes. I believe in the happy medium as far as possible" (M50 El).

"Well, if you go along quietly, doing the right thing all the time" (M55 El).

"Do sufficient work, have a medium of pleasure, and don't take no advantages" (M60 El).

"Have enough to eat and drink and a roof over your head, and have good children" (F45 El).

"Work. Look after those you have to and mind your own

business, I suppose. But I just carry on without thinking about things like this. A good thriller and a roaring fire suits me better than taking or reading this religious stuff" (M35 Sec).

"To do away with ambition and just be content, and to live a fairly average sort of life" (M18 El).

"Oh, a reasonable number of interests, both work and pleasure properly balanced" (M20 Sec).

"By not overworking yourself and taking the best way of having a good time without upsetting anybody" (F35 El).

"Best thing's to live a steady proper life and don't do anyone any harm. And don't feel in any ways covetous of what they've got" (M70 Sec).

With these may be compared the many who said that taking things as they come, not worrying, keeping smiling, were the ways of getting the best from life:

"To take everything practically as it comes and do the best you can" (M45 El).

"Jog along, I should say" (M45 El).

"To take things very steadily and be contented" (M40 El).

"To take it easily and not to take things too seriously" (M55 El: Catholic).

"Take things as they come and don't moan about little things. Don't worry until the time comes" (M20 El).

"To give and take, I suppose. Don't worry over nothing. Take it or let it go" (F35 El).

"I don't know. I think it's just to ignore the small troubles and make the best of your life" (F30 El).

"Dunno. Keep cheerful; enjoy things as they come along" (F18 El).

Don't worry, don't anticipate, don't interfere, don't be too ambitious, don't expect too much—these notes are a recurrent theme. Even some of those who say that being good is the way to get the best from life suggest a basic minimum:

"Abide by the laws of the country, and I can't say anything else. Go contrary to them, and you may get into trouble" (M70 El).

And, from those who suggest work or money as the most important:

"Work, and don't stop to think about it" (F35 El).
"To expect very little and to work very hard" (M35 Sec).
"To have enough money not to worry about it" (M35 Sec).

This sort of outlook is basic among large masses of people. Doubtless, there is nothing new in that, for the great majority must always follow the middle way. Whether they look upon it like the working-class woman who said of the purpose of life:

"I think we're all born with a cross and we've got to grin and bear it, and carry the cross all the time."

or her male counterpart, who said the most important thing in life was "beer and something to look forward to," there is the natural enough tendency not to overdo hope, ambition and expectation, so as to avoid risking too much disappointment. The lack of wide idealisms, concentration on the simple, the immediate, the unorganised personal side, neighbourliness, non-interference; on fun, and money for fun, on keeping clear of too many obligations and ties, keeping the home together and the home relationships bright—these are the normal everyday strivings of most people's lives. Asked, in pre-war days, to say which of ten subjects were the most important for their own personal happiness, Lancashire cotton-workers voted (Mass-Observation survey, worktown):

Security	129
Knowledge	118
Religion (personal and organised)	104
Humour	80
Equality	79
Beauty	34
Action	23
Pleasure	10
Leadership	8
Politics	2

In the present survey too, the almost complete absence of any reference to changing things, working together for causes, political ideals, etc., points the same way. The great gulf which separates the few whose purpose, whose most important thing, whose way of getting the best from life, lies in trying to make life *different for humanity*, is shown by the results of a survey made recently among Mass-Observation National Panel of observers. These people, predominantly middle-class, showing by their membership of Mass-Observation that they are more than normally interested in other people, were asked to write in detail about their aims in life, with the following results:

Aims in Life	Percentage among Middle-class thoughtful Sample saying this is one of Their Aims
Usefulness, "causes," politics, fulfilling function, etc.	46
Individual development, character, spiritual development	23
Family (married people only)	21
Work, interesting jobs, particular jobs	20
Helping others, making others happy, not doing harm	17
Miscellaneous material self-benefiting	16
Mental development, knowledge, theoretical understanding	13
Culture, writing, acting, etc.	12
Money (where purpose not stated, or for comfort, etc.)	11
Full life, varied experience	9
Travel	9
Marriage (or family if unmarried)	8
Happiness	7
Old age (mostly money for; but also memories for, training for)	7
Health	4
Other miscellaneous	8
None (only when no aim mentioned. Some say none, then mention aims)	6

Politics, "causes," and allied interests come top for these people, mentioned twice as often as anything else. This virtually reverses the emphasis of the ordinary citizens of war-time Metrop and the cotton-workers of pre-war Worktown, whose values centre round the smaller circle of home, private life, and personal acquaintance. The contrast is further underlined when we consider the groups in which the "Middle-class intelligent" and the ordinary citizen move.

XV

ORGANISATION

THE NATIONAL PANEL were asked to give a list of all the organisations to which they belonged; and the Metrop sample were run through a list of possible types of organisation and asked whether they belonged to any of each type, or to any other sort. In both cases it was made clear that *any* kind of group counted, and in the following analysis equal weight is given to a local darts team, a football club, or an association of philatelists of which membership is arranged by post and which does not involve any personal meeting between members. Professional associations were mainly trade unions, of which membership does not, of course, necessarily involve any more activity than paying dues. In general the aim was to get at the extent to which people are associated together in any sort of purposeful grouping not of a purely personal nature. The results for the two surveys may be compared:

Number of Organisations beolnged to	Percentage belonging to this Number among	
	"Middle-class intelligent"	Ordinary People
None	20[1]	59
1–2	23	36
3 and over	57	5

Among the special group 30 per cent. were members of six or more organisations, and nearly half of these belonged to nine and over. On the other hand, even among the special group, over two-fifths belong to only none, one or two. Thus, even if we take a group of people who show by their membership of Mass-Observation that they are the sort who *do* join organisations, we find a minority of less than a third holding about two-thirds of the membership cards held by the whole group. There is a minority within a minority of "organisationally-minded" people who go in for group activity in a big way.

[1] Other than Mass-Observation.

They help particularly to swell the membership roll of small organisations and societies with similar aims, one person adding his or her name to six or a dozen membership lists.

How different the picture is outside this special group. In Metrop three people out of five do not belong to any sort of non-personal group at all, and of those who do only one in eight belong to three or more. Breaking down the results by sex, age and education we find:

Group	Percentage of this Group belonging to No Organisation
Men	41
Women	79
Young	56
Old	63
Secondary education	55
Elementary education	61

Four out of five women in Metrop say they do not belong to any sort of organisation, two out of five men. The young and the educated are little more organised than the old and the less educated. Among the whole sample:

59 per cent. belong to no sort of organisation at all.

23 per cent. belong to organisations connected with their recreation, hobbies, games, etc.

22 per cent. belong to trade unions, professional organisations, etc.

5 per cent. belong to organisations connected with the Churches (though not necessarily "religious organisations").

5 per cent. belong to political and similar organisations (though not necessarily active in them).

3 per cent. belong to organisations connected with social service, charity, etc.

2 per cent. belong to other sorts of organisation.

Between one person in four and one in five say they belong to some organisation connected with pleasureful recreation, about the same proportion to some sort of organisation connected with their job. To no other type of organisation does more than one person in twenty belong.

The number of people in the less organised groups is small, so that statistical differences must be large to be of significance. The number of women belonging to any organisation is only a little over fifty, but even on this small sample we can see that there is a considerable difference between the way women and men are organised:

Type of Organisation	Percentage of those who belong to Any Organisation who belong to one of this Type among— Men	Women
Recreation, etc.	61	49
Professional, Trade Union, etc.	60	41
Religious, etc.	5	37
Politics, etc.	16	0
Social service, etc.	2	25
Other	5	0

Women who belong to organisations do so much more than men to those connected with the Churches, social service and charity. In Metrop a practically negligible number of women belong to political organisations.

If we readjust the figures to show the proportion of the whole sample who belong to each kind or organisation, we find:

Type of Organisation	Percentage of Whole Sample belonging to an Organisation of this Type among— Men	Women
Recreation, etc.	37	10
Professional, Trade Union, etc.	36	8
Religious, etc.	3	7
Politics, etc.	10	0
Social service, etc.	1	5
Other	3	0

Men outnumber women by about four to one in recreational and occupational organisations in Metrop; and overwhelmingly in political ones. In social service organisations women outnumber men by five to one, and in societies, etc., connected with the Churches by seven to three.

The young belong to organisations slightly more than the old; but this difference is more than accounted for by the fact that over twice as many belong to recreational groups:

Type of Organisation	Percentage of members who belong to One of this Type among Organisations—	
	Young	Old
Recreation, etc.	77	35
Professional, Trade Union, etc.	53	55
Religious, etc.	7	21
Politics, etc.	9	14
Social service, etc.	3	14
Other	1	9

Expressed as a percentage of all under-forties in Metrop:

4 per cent. belong to an organisation connected with politics.

3 per cent. belong to an organisation connected with religion.

1 per cent. belong to an organisation connected with social service.

The difference between more and less educated people was chiefly that the more educated belonged to more recreational organisations, and rather less to organisations connected with their job. All those who belonged to social service organisations were believers, and so were all but one of those who belonged to organisations connected with the Church; but there was no other significant difference between those who believed in God and didn't.

Leisure, Unorganised

The chief centres of unorganised leisure in Metrop are the pubs and the cinemas. Three-quarters of Metrop people say they have been to the cinema at some time during the past six months, and of these nearly two-thirds have been within a week. Cinema-going works out like this:

Percentage who say they have been to the cinema in the past six months among—					
Men	Women	Young	Old	Secondary Education	Elementary Education
70	77	93	55	73	74

And of these:

Time of Last Visit to Cinema	Men	Women	Young	Old	Elementary Education	Secondary Education
Up to one week ago	62	63	73	48	57	65
Over a week, up to a month	20	21	15	28	24	19
Over a month, up to six months	18	16	12	24	19	16

Percentage of Cinemagoers who they say made their Last Visit this Long Ago among—

A considerable majority of all groups except older people (and more than half of these), go to cinemas. Just as many of the more educated go as of the less educated; but more educated cinemagoers go a little less frequently. The cinemagoing habits of men and women are practically identical, though perhaps slightly more Metrop men than women don't go at all.

Among all groups, of those who go to cinemas at all in Metrop between a half and three-quarters have been within the week. Among the under-forties cinemagoing is practically universal; most of the 7 per cent. who haven't been in the past six months have been prevented from doing so for some reason such as illness, bad eyesight, having babies, etc. They nearly all go unless they are prevented for reasons beyond their control; and three-quarters of them have been during the past week. Though no attempt was made in this survey to find out what proportion go more than once a week, many young people do, and, at a rough estimate probably about two-thirds of the younger generation of Metrop see an average of at least fifty films a year. The sample was not large enough for a further age split to be of any significance, but the signs are there is a pretty steep rise in film going as we go down the age scale. One lad of seventeen—a slater-improver earning 1s. 8d. an hour—discussing his normal leisure habits, said:

"Generally me and the boys go to the pictures and the Globe (music-hall) six times a week. When we come out about 8.30, we go into the funfair in —— Road. We muck about there with the pin-tables and meet the girls—there's a clique of them—and after a bit, we just walk around, or muck about."

Pub-going

Pub-going works out like this:

	Percentage who say they have been to a pub during the past six months among—					
	Men	Women	Young	Old	Elementary Education	Secondary Education
	75	47	65	58	51	64

and of these:

Time of Last visit to a pub	*Percentage of Pub-goers who say they made Their Last Visit this long ago, among*					
	Men	Women	Young	Old	Elementary Education	Secondary Education
Up to one week ago	81	53	65	73	68	69
Over a week, up to a month	10	30	14	19	14	17
Over a month, up to six months	9	27	21	8	18	14

Three-quarters of the men, and rather less than half of the women, in Metrop say they go to pubs. Not only do more of the men go, but those who go do so much more regularly. About a quarter of women pub-goers go only half a dozen times or less in a year. This is probably special to the area one of high pub concentration.

Rather more young people than old go to pubs, but the young pub-goers go considerably less frequently than the old.

Although more people with secondary education don't go to pubs at all than those with elementary education, there is little difference in the frequency with which those that do go frequent the pubs.

Thus both pub-going and cinema-going are done by more of the young than the old. So far as cinema-going is concerned, not only do many more young people go, but they go much more frequently. Once a week or more is routine with a very clear majority of the under-forties in Metrop. In pub-going the younger generation have caught up with their elders— more of them go, though they don't go so regularly. However, there are signs that the young women, at any rate, are fairly rapidly making good this deficiency. A survey made in 1943 in a neighbouring borough showed that, among women aged under thirty, nine said they were going to pubs more often than before the war for every one who said she was going less often. Young men, on the other hand, had not changed their habits much.[1]

In general, both in organised activity and these main facets of unorganised leisure, we find the men and young people concentrating on pleasure, either of an active or passive kind, comparatively and absolutely few of them concerned with organisations to do with social affairs, other people, activities with a non-recreational purpose. The indications are, moreover, that the differences which we have pointed out between the under-forties and over-forties would be equally pronounced if we contrasted the fifteen to twenty-five age group with the twenty-five to thirty-five. Despite the big wartime drive to get young people into a variety of organised activities, London youth is probably less organised than ever? Comparative figures for pre-war, blitz-time 1941, and spring, 1943, among the age-group fourteen to twenty in a London borough (not Metrop) show:

Time	Proportion of Young People age fourteen to twenty who said They belonged to any kind of Organisation at this Time Per cent.
Prewar	32
January, 1941 (London blitz)	25
January, 1943	37

In 1943 a fifth of youth in the borough belonged to A.T.C., G.T.C. and other war organisations. The apparent increase is entirely due to this. Only one in seven in 1943 belonged to non-war organisations, and if we adjust the 1943 results according to the known pre-war membership of clubs, etc., it seems that a comparable figure to those obtained before the establishment of the military organisations would be around a fifth—even lower than the blitz-time figure. In other words, young people who have grown up during the

[1] One way of looking at many of the attitude and habit-changes which have taken place over recent years would be to say that people generally are thinking and behaving more like young men.

war are becoming de-organised even in regard to their recreational interests. Conversely, unorganised leisure-pleasures are on the increase. The cinema-a-week routine is established among the majority of a whole generation in Metrop, but it is quite possible that the routine of the generation now coming to maturity will be two or three cinemas a week. With regard to pub-going, the 1943 survey showed that about two-fifths of youth in the other borough go to pubs, and most of these go pretty regularly. Since half that sample were below the legal age for visiting pubs, the majority of those who have grown up during the war seem, in this borough, to be forming a pretty regular pub-going routine as soon as it is legal for them to do so.

Churchgoing and cinemagoing were compared with belief in a Deity. Substantially more of the non-believers than of the believers are pub-goers, and rather more are cinemagoers; but these differences are accounted for by age and sex factors.

The information given by this survey does not reveal any difference between the organised and unorganised leisure activities of believers and non-believers, other than those which directly reflect the known differences between young and old, men and women. This, we have seen, is true of most points investigated. There are certain attitudes associated particularly with the younger generation and the male sex which are also found predominantly among non-believers. Since non-believers are predominantly young and male this in itself does not get us very far. The young, male, non-believer attitude and focus may be characterised as less co-operative, more personal-pleasureful. In previous chapters we have shown that membership of organised religious bodies is more strongly associated with "interdependent," broadly speaking co-operative attitudes, than would be expected if only age-sex factors were responsible for the association. We cannot base any very positive conclusions on these facts, but we can point out the absence of any sign that the decay of religious faith is associated with *new* standards or activities of a broadly co-operative kind.

If a new ethic is arising among those who doubt the existence of a Deity it is an ethic of "independence," not only of

God, but of other people, a concentration on more purely personal aims and pleasures—not necessarily more "selfish," for characteristic believers' attitudes often show self-interests consciously enough recognised at no distant remove. What we can say is : religious beliefs are declining most among the same groups that are most inclined to "make their own life," ostensibly to rely least on others and to expect others to rely least on them. Overlying is the wider pleasure-independence trend; and underlying is the very general verbal adherence to some of the simpler ethical teachings of Christianity, and its residual memories, largely derived from childhood and adolescence.

XVI

PROGRESS AND SCIENCE

"Mankind's progressing to destroying itself, I should say."
"I think we're going round in circles."
"We're going forward, though not in the right direction."
"Progress is a spiral."
"It's progressing in a technical way But I don't see that anybody could hold the view that it's getting better."
"We're progressing too much."

When people were asked whether they considered mankind was progressing or not, replies showed the extraordinarily mixed connotations attached to the word "progress." About one person in twelve said, in effect: "Yes, we're going forwards—backwards," culminating in the comment of the young man who said: "We're progressing forward to degradation every day."

Numerically opinions were as follows:

Attitude to Progress	Percentage expressing this Attitude among			
	Men	Women	Both	
Mankind is progressing	49	38	43	
Tend to think this	3	9	6	49
Mankind not progressing	19	19	19	
Tend to think this	4	2	3	
Mankind "progressing backwards"	10	6	8	30
Progressing in some ways, not in others	9	4	7	
Undecided	6	22	14	21

Had this question been asked on a crude ballot form a considerably larger proportion of people would have been found saying that mankind *is* progressing. For the very word progress has come to mean to many people nothing more than technical innovation, change, for good or for bad. It is thus possible for people to say they think mankind is progressing and mean nothing more by it than that new things are being invented. In the above analysis those who said this and showed by their comments that "progress" to them seemed to be leading to disaster, to be leading in the wrong direction, to have got out of hand, were grouped with those who thought mankind was *not* progressing. In other words comments were judged not simply by a formal yes or no, but by their implicit attitude towards progress. The effect of the different meanings people have for the word is thus partially eliminated, which is essential in order to obtain any quantitative indications. But even then 30 per cent. is probably a low estimate for the proportion of people who definitely feel that mankind is *not* progressing, or that progress has become a bad thing.

As we have already pointed out, questioning on such a broad subject can only measure the top level of already crystallised reaction. The deep and still unformulated anxiety and confusion, is not approachable in this simple, quantitative way. Only presently will it rise to the explicit, expressed, verbal level. With the possible exception of rather more cynicism among more educated people, scepticism about progress seems to be distributed pretty equally among all groups covered by this survey.

Those who said mankind was progressing were then asked in what ways they thought it was doing so:

Way in which Mankind is Progressing	Percentage saying Mankind is progressing in this Way among—		
	Men	Women	Both
Science	40	18	30
Social improvements, standard of living, medicine . . .	19	23	21
Education, mentally . . .	17	11	15
Kinder, better	10	4	7
Everything	11	14	12
Other ways	13	13	13
Don't know	6	29	17

Women were much less able to say why they thought

mankind was progressing than men, and were much less inclined than men to speak of scientific progress.

There was no significant difference between the replies of old and young. Those with elementary education were slightly more inclined than those with secondary education to see progress in terms of education, but the difference was not great. Non-believers mentioned educational progress rather more than believers.

Those who said mankind was not progressing were asked why they thought so. They replied as follows:

Reason for thinking Mankind is not progressing	\multicolumn{3}{c}{Percentage giving this as Their Reason for thinking Mankind is not progressing among—}
	Men	Women	Both
War, abuse of science, etc.	46	50	48
Less kind, less good	18	20	19
Other comments	32	24	28
Don't know	9	8	8

The number of people saying mankind is not progressing is too small for group differences to mean much here, but it is worth noticing that only a tenth of young people, compared with a quarter of old, say it is not progressing because it is getting less kind or less good; and only 4 per cent. of non-believers, compared with 23 per cent. of believers say this. The nature of the verbatim comments does, as we shall see, show that many of those replying in this way are in fact comparing the general social atmosphere as they remember it in their youth unfavourably with the social atmosphere to-day.

Science and Progress

In a general way, the categories used here to describe the ways in which people think the world *is* progressing are self-explanatory. They look upon progress in the familiar and by now traditional light, as an amalgam of scientific invention, social improvement, and increased knowledge and educational opportunity. About half are moderately or strongly decided that this sort of process is going on, and that it is for the best. Not much is gained by quoting their views. We are concerned here with analysing the attitude of the "disillusioned third" who deviate from the traditional attitude, and who are expressing the less traditional view, so that they are probably themselves leaders in a progressive train of doubt.

Typical of the less specific comments of those who thought mankind was not progressing were:

"Oh yes, it's progressing. Progressing a bit too far. There's no end to inventing things, particularly of the instruments to destroy life" (M35 El).

"Well, the wars have put us back for a start. And again people put the value on the wrong things. I might say we've progressed in the wrong kind of things" (M18 El).

Many think that science is "progressing" too fast:

"I wouldn't say it's exactly to the right ends. Science is too advanced. At the moment it seems dreadful, doesn't it? Just killing one another" (F30 Sec).

"I think we're progressing too fast and the war's pulled us up and made us stop and think in what a senseless way we're using all the best of the world's brains and money. I think it's given us something to think about" (M60 Sec).

"We're advancing in science. We're going forward there. Sometimes I think we're getting to the stage of advancing too far" (M65 Sec).

"Well, yes and no. It's progressing faster than I like as regards science. It's like a kid playing with matches. But it's not progressing in its mind; far from it" (M50 El).

Some said not only that science was progressing too fast, but that the results of progress made things move too fast:

"Progressing too much, I think. I don't think it's natural for everything to be so mechanical. We're crazy for greed and speed. Things move too quickly. It's unnatural. We're overstepping in some ways" (F45 El).

"Mankind will actually kill itself in the end. Man'll kill man in the long run. We're progressing too quickly. Take the flying bomb speed. The fastest speed of the aeroplane was 300 m.p.h. Well, look at it now; the flying bomb can travel at 700 m.p.h. Well, we're progressing too fast, and in the end it will kill us" (M35 El).

For many people the idea of progress has become dissociated from any idea of whether the change is for the good of mankind or not. As one old man put it:

"Well, it's certainly progressing, even in war—bigger and better everything. If the purpose of wars is to slaughter people, then this war shows progress. The heathen with his bow and arrow; we used to laugh at him, but now he's got the laugh of us" (M60 El).

And similarly those who said we were progressing in the wrong way or progressing towards destruction:

"It certainly is in a scientific manner, but it's progressing on the wrong lines. They can't even cure the common cold. If they studied to do that instead of all these fancy explosions, well we'd all be better off" (M65 El).

"Oh yes, it'll progress, but it'll destroy itself" (M16 El).

"Oh yes, progressing, only in the wrong way" (M20 El).

"Yes, but only to their own eventual destruction" (F35 Sec).

To these must be added the people who, looking upon progress as something intrinsically to mankind's good, see no signs of progress:

"It gets worse and worse. The more inventions there are the more they are used for devastation instead of creation all the time" (F30 Sec).

"Definitely not. I think we're going backwards as fast as we possibly can" (F25 Sec).

"If we're progressing, why do men go and kill themselves? It's always been the same as far as yesterday goes. It's the same now as it was in the first place" (M35 El).

"Well, I don't know. That often makes me wonder, too. Well, you look around with the war on and they call it civilisation. It would be all right if the inventions were for good, not evil. But somebody invents something and someone else tries to see how they can kill each other with it" (F30 El).

"No, I think the last twenty years has seen a breakdown in the human conscience without parallel in any age since the Middle Ages" (M35 Sec).

It may be objected with some justification that this sort of attitude is only to be expected in the midst of world worry, and that what is remarkable is not so much the fact that one person in three feels this way as that half feel mankind *is* progressing. But this does not make the prevalence of such feelings to-day any less significant for the future. One possible repercussion is seen in occasional comments of this sort:

"I think we're doing too much thinking. We're meddling too much in things we ought not to" (M50 El).

"In one way yes, in one way no. I think it's getting so darned clever it'll soon wipe itself off the earth, if you call that progress" (M50 El).

"I believe it's all these inventions that are man's undoing" (F40 El).

The feeling that the repercussions of invention are getting out of hand comes out occasionally as a belief that machinery itself is somehow at the back of present-day troubles:

"This machine, we're not using it in the right way. In olden times, when the work was done by hand, people felt better and lived longer. Nowadays we've got all this machinery that's supposed to ease life, and what do we find but people rushing about more. We're worse off in the long run" (F50 El).

And two eighteen-year-old lads at a factory:

"We're progressing too much. We're sort of relying too much on machinery. It's spoiling the health of the people."

"Take these inventions in machinery. That man there, he's working on a machine that normally employs eight people; now it will only employ two. I don't know about jobs for all—there'll be so many out of work as a result of man's inventions."

Back of all this it is not difficult to discern a suspicion that the world might be a better place without all this science and invention, cleverness and thinking. In Metrop we found some indication that scepticism about progress was found more among people with secondary education than others: 40 per cent. of the more educated people doubted whether mankind was progressing, compared with 26 per cent. of those with only an elementary education. As we have seen people's ideas of progress centre round science, an investigation made earlier in the war among the National Panel is of considerable interest in assessing the attitudes of a more than averagely informed section of the community.

The panel, being members of Mass-Observation, might be expected to show a considerably more favourable attitude to science than most. In fact, if one wanted to select a sample biased in favour of science the members of a scientific organisation would seem an excellent selection. They were asked to describe their normal everyday attitudes to science, and a numerical analysis of replies gave the following results, practically identical for men and women:

Normal Everyday Attitude to Science	Percentage saying this is Their Attitude
Unqualified favourable attitudes	20
With qualifications on lack of control or application, not blaming the scientist	46
Lack of control or application seen as scientists' responsibility	6
Other moderately anti-science attitudes	5
Strong anti-science attitudes	7
Indifferent	5
Undecided, half and half	5
Unclassified	6

There was one overwhelmingly prominent attitude, colouring appreciation of what science has done and what it may do in the future—the feeling that science has got out of control. Though most people, among this specialised sample, do not think that this is the scientists' fault, but rather that of the community or unscrupulous, unspecified, non-scientists; though most of them do not show a distrust of the scientific approach, way of thought, or of science in general; nevertheless a very appreciable minority of about 18 per cent. do hold such attitudes. Let us examine people's comments in more detail. First of all there is the feeling that man's knowledge has outstripped his spiritual development and that he is losing control of the way knowledge is applied and used:

"My general feeling is that, whilst in some ways, as in the growth of medical knowledge, etc., the findings of science have been turned to good account, on the whole it has been misused, as in the development of poison gases, weapons of war, etc. I suppose that the root of the trouble is that the development of science has far outstripped man's moral and spiritual development—that he resembles a child playing with highly dangerous toys."

"Science has done tremendous things for the world so far. What it is probably doing is to outstrip man's moral control, and the repercussions resulting therefrom will have their effects in due course. Unless man can rise to the occasion and develop his soul as well as his brain, maladjustments will be amplified and civilisation will take (if not already) a downward trend."

Overlying people's attitudes there is an almost mystical sense of science as the potential universal panacea. Phrases like the following abound:

"I regard science as the one reliable thing in the world. . . ."

"I feel that science and its discoveries are the most thrilling thing in these times. . . ."

"Science. The outpost of intelligence. . . ."

"I believe that far too few people realise that science in future must save the world, if it can be saved. . . ."

"A marvellous and completely unintelligible miracle or machine. . . ."

"I believe . . . that a belief in science—that is, the search for God's truth—will eventually lead us to the only God we are ever likely to put our faith in. . . ."

"Science terrifies me, bewilders me. When I contemplate, in the limited way I am able to observe, the marvels of science, I am appalled by my own insignificance. . . ."

There is the feeling that science, with its enormous complications and specialisations, is a power essentially outside the ordinary person's ken. But underlying, and arising directly from this uncomprehending wonderment and awe, the feeling that science is doing things, so to speak, independently of man, and is liable to take control:

> "Science has made literature and knowledge, wit and music, available to all. It has the potentiality to turn man from beast to God. It also has the potentiality to turn man into a brain in a bottle. We cannot put the clock back now. Mechanisation must proceed to its logical conclusion, and I believe that drudgery will disappear. But having no work to do we are in danger of extinction through boredom and vice. How to utilise leisure? That is the problem of the future which must be solved or we shall be exterminated. We must help ourselves or we shall be steam-rollered by the irresistible juggernaut of science."

Many are worried because they feel that scientific thought and its applications are taking possession of the field, and one side of man's nature is being left out of account:

> "... There is a danger of science becoming a sort of deity. There is more in the world than scientific data. It is all a question of balance, and it should not be difficult to achieve. By taking advantage of all the help they can give us without turning us into automatons."

> "I believe that scientific mass-production as we know it now is the root of our present trouble. It has made our minds mass-produced as well as everything else so that we have no individuality left and move all the time as an immense crowd swayed by whoever's clever enough to do it. . . ."

> "I feel that science is running to seed. Science is continually evolving new theories and new ideas, all of which tend to reduce man's powers of resistance by making him dependent on external forces. His own powers of initiative are sapped and man, as a race, becomes weaker. . . ."

These comments may be compared with those of Metrop people who feel that "progress" is not making people any happier. As two elderly men put it:

"In some ways the standard of living's gone up, but people aren't so contented in a body. Before, when all wages were low the cost of living was cheap and entertainment was limited. When I was young we used to go cycling and for walks, and a weekly visit to the music-hall was the extent of our entertainment. Apart from that, we depended on ourselves. And it promoted a good deal of family friendship which I think is a good thing. Nowadays people have no idea of family life. In this factory there are about 4,000 people, all hoping to be married, and when they are married they carry on work here and regard home as some place to sleep. It isn't only wartime; it was happening before the war" (M55 El).

"Not progressing in the last twenty years, are they? I don't believe it is. We're going back. Thirty years ago two workmen was different from each other. Ten times more sociable. The conditions is affecting them. Take the valleys. The more I think it's human beings are not so sociable, but more independent" (M60 El).

In their varied ways all these attitudes are sceptical of "progress"—in the commonly used sense of new invention and scientific discovery—getting mankind anywhere. Taken together, the sorts of outlook which we have described here are those of a large number of people, ranging from the intellectual who feels that "science" is reducing everyone on to a soulless mass level, to the apprentice who believes that machinery is taking away his chances of employment. The possible outcome of such an outlook is seen in the remarks of those who say that mankind is getting too clever, thinking too much. It is not such a far step to shift the blame for the misuse of scientific knowledge on to those who are responsible for unearthing it. An observer reports:

"Mr. X. is firm in his belief that all scientists should be hung by the neck until dead and then left as a grisly warning to others. This procedure, he states, is necessary to stem the spate of horrible things which flow from their laboratory benches in the form of bombs, germs, gases, and all the thousand and one technicalities designed to destroy and/or impede the progress of civilisation. . . . Mr. X. would also like to see the aeroplane inventors and technicians enjoying a similar fate to the science-mongers."

And a chemist:

"The strange idea is prevalent that the misuse of material and power which science has made possible is the responsibility of science (i.e. the would world be better with less science). . . ."

Scepticism about science and progress are growing alongside scepticism about the religious beliefs which science first queried. But there is no sign to-day that the two scepticisms are connected. Some are losing one belief, some another, and some both. But there can be little doubt that faith in God, progress and science are all weakening. It may seem a far cry from these scepticisms to the burning of the books, but Mr. X.'s proposal to save the future by hanging the inventors and technicians is ominously suggestive. Once people have reached the stage of thinking that the evils of to-day have arisen *because* men have thought too much, it is not far to a belief that the world would be better if they were forced to think less. Science has a lot of ground to make up if it is to regain the respect it once had. And, in part at least, the process will be dependent on the scientists themselves. If scientific methods and inventions are again applied in ways which seem to ordinary people to be leading to less overall happiness for mankind, the signs are that ordinary people will reject the plea that "science" is not responsible for the way it's used. To the scientist particularly, the suggestion that he should be held responsible for the way the results of his research are used may seem specious. But private emotional overtones are often finally decisive in public feeling, and there is a good deal of emotion prevalent about "science" to-day.

XVII

CLERGY'S VIEWS

AFTER THE GENERAL TRENDS arising from this investigation had become clear, clergymen of the various Churches and leaders of youth clubs in Metrop were interviewed informally to see how their impressions compared with those we had arrived at. A little of this material has already been presented incidentally. Some of the rest is now relevant.

Aims

Clergy were mostly agreed in saying that, in their experience, most people were very vague about their aims and objects in life. Some put this down to the insecurity of past years, the habit of living from day to day:

"I don't think people have any really definite aims in life. I think it's because they have been living so long with the expectation of war that there didn't seem to be much point in making plans about the future. And now the problems of everyday life absorb them so much that there isn't time for people to think much about abstract things" (Church of England Vicar).

"On the whole I should think people are only concerned with the present moment nowadays—they're living for the day only, in a hand to mouth sort of way" (Church of England Vicar).

Some thought that people were feeling the need of a more definite purposefulness:

"I think they feel the lack of one very much, and the more since the war—it's frightened them—jerked them out of their comfortable little rut in the suburbs" (Methodist Minister).

"They don't think about it at all, I should say, until an emergency comes. Then they begin to think" (Presbyterian Minister).

"Well, now, they're very vague about it, but underlying everything there's a very deep and very serious need" (Methodist).

There seemed a certain scepticism underlying the comments of several of the clergy, as if they were saying that the problem was really too big for them to do much about it. It was sad, but there it was. One Church of England priest who said in the course of conversation: "I think music a substitute for religion. People get the same sort of feeling from listening to music," commented on people's aims in life:

"I don't think people have any definite aims in life. I think that's what's the matter these days. I think they'd be much better if they had. They are so occupied with the little things they haven't time for any further thought."

But he volunteered no spontaneous information on what he felt the Church could do about it, and talking of the decrease in congregation: "I don't see how anything could be done about it."

For the general vagueness about aims and the lack of religious background clergymen widely blamed the educational system. Many felt strongly about it, though their ideas ranged from the suggestion that children should be given a general philosophy of life, to a belief that the problem will not be solved until all denominations exercise their own denominational instruction. Here are some typical comments:

"There's no doubt that the majority of people don't know what the Christian faith is. Much of it is just memories of childhood teaching. You can't teach children as you can grown people—you tell them Bible stories and so on, and that probably accounts for their confusion now—they've never faced up to it as adults" (Church of England).

"I think the confused attitude is accounted for by it being all they hazily remember of what they were taught at Sunday school, or half-remembering stories they learned as children. And before the age of fourteen children can't have a real understanding of what religion means" (Methodist).

"Most people believe in God. A person isn't an atheist

because he doesn't believe in Christ. But their beliefs don't have much effect as a rule until an emergency comes along. I think the majority of people are religious, but that's not to say they're churchgoers. The religion they get taught in schools isn't very much. I find a lot of people who are very anxious for their children to go to Sunday school—they want some minimum grounding, but after that they let it slide" (Presbyterian).

"Well, I've thought for years that the education in Board schools and secondary schools and probably others doesn't furnish an adequate philosophy of life, with the result that people leave school with no adequate interpretation of life. I should doubt whether people would actually *say* they needed an aim in life but I think they're groping for one and don't know where to look for it" (Baptist).

"Unless you have some dogma or doctrine that has the authority not of men's notions but of divine revelation, I don't see how you can expect anything but confusion—a divine revelation we can't tamper with or change. The present mistake is in asking what *men* would like; the question is what *God* would like. . . . Christianity is supposed to be the national religion, but people's attitude is that any old religion will do. As long as we as an establishment stand, we have the right to expect that the schools of the country will teach the children definite Christian doctrine, and, failing that, every denomination should have the right to teach the children what the parents wish it to know. But the Government is terrified of Labour and so on, and of course not convinced themselves. But you can't run a world on trade union pacts and financial contracts. Man has a spirit and a soul. Even dear old Churchill now talks of Christian civilisation, and he used only to talk about civilisation" (Anglo-Catholic).

Thus there is wide agreement among the clergy of various denominations interviewed that, in their specialised experience, people to-day are not at all clear about their aims in life, and that, so far as religious outlooks play their part, aimlessness and confusion can largely be attributed to inadequate instruction in schools. The notable exception was a Catholic youth leader, who said:

"I should say that most of my youngsters know what they're here for, and even though they're too young to have a fixed aim, the fundamental ideas are fixed and have been from early childhood. That's the most impressive thing people notice in favour of religious education controlled by the Roman Catholic church; and these children I would say are far more easy to handle in an organised club than the products of other educational systems. You don't have to start from scratch if you know what I mean. You have definitely got youngsters with a background of the spiritual."

The same man said of the organisation of the Catholic religion:

"The only properly organised religion is the Roman Catholic. You could hardly call the slap-dash methods applied to religious teaching by the unrecognised Churches as organised. The Roman Catholic is the original Church of Christ, and in countries such as this one and America, where attempts are made to ignore the authority of the Pope, you can hardly expect the young people to take much interest in the substitutes put forward by well-meaning but ignorant dignitaries."

There seems to be very little between the extremes of satisfaction with efficient indoctrination and dissatisfaction with inadequate elementary instruction.

Attitudes to the Church

We have said that there seemed to be some scepticism among some of the clergy interviewed about their own capacity to do anything much towards changing people's attitudes. This came out most clearly when they were asked how they would describe the attitude of ordinary people to organised religion and the Church. They generally replied that people were indifferent; not opposed, but simply not interested:

"As I go around the parish I don't find opposition, just luke-warmness and indifference" (Church of England).

"A certain hostility, mainly directed to the Church of England, because they're supposed to be the bastions of capitalism and a money-making racket. Otherwise there's indifference—they think about churchgoing as a sort of harmless hobby. I think there's a void in them that isn't filled. If they imagine religion is an explanation of the mysteries of life, well, they leave it. They think science has explained everything. The void isn't intellectual, it's much deeper . . ." (Methodist).

"Generally speaking, one of indifference. It's not hostile at all—they're quite willing to make use of you when they need you" (Presbyterian).

"I think a large number of them feel that organised religion isn't effective—it doesn't make itself felt—and of course they love the line of the Church of England owning slum property. The attitude is, let my neighbour go to church if he wants to, but I prefer to potter about at home —we're all free to do as we like" (Baptist).

This widespread indifference without ill-will must be exceedingly irksome, and several clergymen were a little sarcastic about the attitude of their parishioners. One Church of England Vicar characterised them this way:

"Eighty per cent. of my parish look upon this church as an institution that provides treats and gives them certain material benefits. Unfortunately, this parish has been noted for immense things done for young people in the past. We've got a large fund for their benefit of which I'm the trustee, and it used to provide outings and so on, done in style. Now there isn't much we can do, except to send sick children away to the country—that sort of thing. It comes to their help in various ways, chiefly material. Hospital letters, filling up forms and so on. ' 'Ere's the bloke wot goes round wiv a cart,' they used to say about me. After the Harvest Festival I used to load the things up on a cart and drive round distributing it. I think they're willing to accept all the help they can get, as long as it commits them to nothing."

Certainly the clergy of Metrop seem to be under no illusion about the status of organised religion in the borough. One gets the impression from their comments that some feel decidedly thwarted and not a little disillusioned. In the midst of this wide indifference, the individual priest may nevertheless be greatly overworked. An Anglican Vicar said:

> "Definitely congregations aren't what they were. You can take the easy comforting explanation if it suits you that these things go in cycles—a falling off and then a revival. Some people console themselves with that. Of course you always get those parrot-like phrases from people time after time: 'Well, I don't go to church. I can worship God quite as well in the open.'
>
> "I came into the church in the slump after the last war. It wasn't too popular. I have to take nine services every Sunday. It's too much. Just imagine having to say the Lord's prayer fourteen fifteen times in one day. And the sacraments too. I had the advantage once of being a layman, and I enjoyed Communion, but you can't imagine how different it is having to officiate. . . ."

Another Vicar made the interesting suggestion that organised religion should be rationalised:

> "Well, my own pet theory is that the man-power of the Church is wasted at present—there's one little parish with a small congregation and another next door to it, and each works singlehanded at his own little patch. What we want is several clergy working together in one Church and a big congregation. It takes us all our time to keep up with the routine work. I personally preach five or six sermons and addresses a week, and it means I'm pretty well run dry, working single-handed, and most of the clergy now are in the same position. The trouble is there are too many churches. Sixty or seventy years ago they went mad on building churches. But of course nobody likes to see their own church closed, though that may be more sentimentalism than anything else. The best way to build up a church is to threaten to close it. . . . The truth is that we're over-organised. We struggle to keep things going to the best of our power."

A Baptist minister, though he did not seem quite comfortable about the idea, was nevertheless impressed by the results of a simple, popular evangelism:

"A friend of mine over at K., the Baptist minister there—he was a football player, splendid athlete and sportsman; then he got converted, and he's now a minister of the Church—a very evangelical preacher, an expert at putting the evangelical appeal—perhaps a rather cheap evangelical appeal too. But the fact is that he's getting more people than all the rest of us put together. He's making the most effective appeal on the score of members. Fine, keen, intelligent *young* folk, too. Perhaps after all the church has something to learn from that kind of work. His church only holds 300, but he's getting all the young folk of sixteen and seventeen and twenty, and his church is packed out every Sunday. I asked him down here to talk to my own young people. He gave a very simple address, but he did it in a very forceful way—effective language, and he puts it across. In comparison our services are cold, and he gets *warmth* into it. That's the secret if we could get at it: warmth."

A Methodist minister also spoke of the coldness of formal religion, which he said had little appeal. He emphasised the importance of communicating a personal experience from individual to individual, spoke of four factory girls "whose whole time had been spent in dancing and drinking cocktails —absolutely devoid of religious knowledge, wholly ignorant of how to behave in church even," who, after an hour in the manageress's office, surrendered their life to Jesus Christ:

"Men and women are not attracted by the Church as such. But when Christianity as a personal issue and a power for life is presented to them they're deeply interested. The cold creed and formal worship has little appeal for anybody. But living Christian fellowship within it is related to life. The New Testament theology was written afterwards. We've a meeting every Thursday, both men and women, whose lives have been completely changed. Business men, department managers, teachers, nurses, whose whole life is radically changed when they come into a personal Christian experience, by meeting with people to whom it is a living thing. It's the living cell propagating."

And another Church of England Vicar in Metrop says he tries to work on the lines of the Moral Rearmament pamphlet, *Battle together for Britain*. This pamphlet is printed throughout in red and blue on white paper. Unlike most religious booklets, the cover gives no indication of its subject. Under the title, to left and right of a blue battleship churning the waves, the symbolic faceless figures of businessmen, office girl, farmer, housewife and factory hand face the reader saluting. In the thirty pages of copiously illustrated text God and religion do not appear till p. 13. The centre spread, stretching straight across two pages reads:

WHAT YOU CAN DO [Red]
BRITAIN NEEDS GUTS AS WELL AS GUNS
NATIONAL CHARACTER IS THE CORE OF NATIONAL STRENGTH
PARLIAMENT [picture of Houses of Parliament] CAN'T VOTE IT
MONEY [picture of money-bags] WON'T BUY IT
IT'S YOUR JOB TO BUILD IT
HOW? [Blue]
CHANGE! UNITE! FIGHT! [Red]

God is introduced on the following page: "Our fathers looked to God for their direction. We've looked almost everywhere else." His name appears eight times on that and the following page, once on the next. On the next two pages not at all, and thereafter once in connection with the king (by the Grace of God, Defender of the Faith). In the marching song, "Battle together for Britain," the words and music of which cover three pages, it occurs once, in the second verse. The booklet ends with the statement that "This handbook comes to you inspired by those who see in its programme of Sound Homes, Teamwork in Industry and a United Nation the basis of a national philosophy for Britain."

We are not here concerned with the philosophy, ethics or religion of the Moral Rearmament movement. The point of interest here is the technique of presentation. The booklet uses the methods of commercial advertising to attain conviction, to sell the idea of God. Like the publicity films which do not introduce the advertised product until the last moment, it builds up the reader's acquiescence before it mentions religion. Moreover it does not say a great deal about God, and its sponsors present their ideas not as religion but as "the basis of a National philosophy." At the other end of the scale of the indirect approach to religion is the alleged project, mentioned by another Metrop parson, for building a church in the centre of London complete with swimming pool, sports facilities, etc.

All these symptoms point in much the same direction—religion with God relegated to the background, the stress on everyday actions, general principles of behaviour, belief in standards of behaviour acquired through personal experience of the need for standards; a philosophy rather than a theology, a coherent way of life rather than a faith. Though of the Moral Rearmament "philosophy" it may be said that God's guidance is the centre, it is presented with the accent off God. First is presented the contemporary need for a faith—material security is not enough. Secondly, a three-point programme—Sound Homes, Teamwork in Industry, a United Nation. Thirdly, an elaboration of these points—"Sound homes put unity into the community." "The true battleline is not between labour and management. It is between the constructive forces and the destructive forces—in each." "Unity is more than agreeing on what we like or whom we like. It is not a question of *who's* right but *what's* right." Fourthly, it is suggested that something new is needed—"We need a new spirit in the country. But to get it we must start with a new spirit in every citizen. And that means you." Then, and only then, God, the theoretical centre but the effectual parenthesis. And the chorus of the march tune with which the booklet ends is this:

> "*You can battle for Britain,*
> *You've something to do,*
> *Clean up the nation from bottom to top,*
> *Start with yourself in the home and the shop!*

> *Battle together for Britain,*
> *Nobody will if you don't!*
> *So get going and give,*
> *And we'll all learn to live*
> *To battle for Britain with you."*

We have already shown that to many ordinary people religion has come to mean simply "good" actions. God is there as a background sanction in their mind, not very important except in crisis, not much thought about, but in the last analysis the *only* sanction many people have for living the way they consider the right way to live.

We have discussed the Moral Rearmament pamphlet at some length because its general gist and sequence of thought conform—in a way which will seem alarming or comforting according to the reader's personal views—so closely to the sort of outlook which many people have to-day. A feeling that something's gone wrong somewhere, that material progress and the efficiencies of science aren't leading to Utopia but away from it, that the old stabilities are stable no longer, that the panaceas and the programmes, politicians and prominents, don't hold out a really great deal of hope for effective, basic change.

Overlying, to-day, an extreme and very conscious concentration on the need for material amenity and security. Underlying, the need for mental and spiritual security, an aim and focus in life that holds together. Superficially, there is a highly realistic attitude to the problems which face the world and this country now that the European war is over. Most people are dissatisfied with things as they are, and were. Most people want basic change, and most are probably more aware than they have ever been before of just what changes they would like to happen. Minds run up and down the scale of material amenity at home, security—personal, national and international—over the changes they believe would make life fairer, safer, easier, less anxious. Superficially, listening to people talking in street, pub, home and barrack room, one may at first get the idea that their broad future target is fixed pretty firmly and definitely. They know what they want and don't want. They know that it won't be easy to achieve even the first semblance of their better Britain; they know this time that there's no easy post-war Utopia to sit and wait for. Yet behind this clarification of the issues, this unprecedented lack of wishful-thinking about the future, there is an inertness, a lack of drive and personal impetus to get going, a breakdown of conviction at the point where it leads forward from talk and disgruntlement to action and hope.

In August, 1944, Mass-Observation reported the result of an enquiry into the use of the proxy-voting form then being distributed to the Forces. It showed the extreme inertness of men and women in uniform over filling in a form which entitled them to vote at the next election. From the evidence collected, mainly from units stationed in this country, we concluded that this lack of initiative could not be put down to just lack of interest and apathy. There were some signs of apathy, but the basic idea was "whoever you vote for you'll get the same thing, so what's the use of voting." The article which we wrote summarising the results of the investigation (*Picture Post*, August 19th) was editorially sub-titled: "This is one of the most disturbing short articles we have ever published." Yet, for anyone who has been in touch with the development of public feeling and mood over the past six years, there is nothing surprising in the affair of the voting form. It simply presented, under clinical conditions, the difference between knowing what's wrong and believing in a way of putting it right. It is the latter which is at a premium to-day.

We reported for the home-based forces; but information received later confirmed that a similar trend was found among those stationed abroad. Here are two reports from officers who were concerned in encouraging people to give themselves the right to vote. First, from India:

"My experience with the voting form is as follows. I'm unit education officer here with about fifteen B.O.R.'s. When notice of the form appeared in I.A. Orders, I republished it on unit notice-boards, and indented for forms. Only one enquiry was made during this period. When forms arrived (fairly promptly) I notified all B.O.R.'s accordingly and then, out of curiosity, didn't try to sell the idea at all. The same N.C.O. immediately filled in his form and dispatched it within twenty-four hours. From the others not one single enquiry was made for the next two weeks. After I devoted the entire next A.B.C.A. period to telling them what I thought of them. Effective result—twelve more forms filled in and eventually dispatched. Conclusions. Main fault is the apathy of the soldier not the War Office. Agreed War Office could 'plug' the idea more rather than coldly announce the existence and purpose of the proxy form. But what *lasting* effect will that have? If people have to be not only given a vote but urged to use it, what kind of citizens are they likely to become?"

That is one way of interpreting the facts—apathy, disinterest. If this were all, if people simply didn't care about who ran the country and how it was run, the future outlook for democracy would certainly seem desperate. But here is another angle, from an officer in Italy:

"In my own case I had the job of A.B.C.A. officer and devoted half of a weekly one-hour period to explaining what it was all about, why and how. This produced very little response, and I tried again later and asked why. The general opinion was that (*a*): 'Whatever we do or say or vote, Big Business, "they," will still and will always run the country as they think fit and not to our advantage necessarily'; and (*b*): 'There are no candidates worth voting for and the Labour Party never do anything when they are in.' They weren't going to vote Communist or I.L.P. (apart from individuals) and Commonwealth candidates were too few for it to be worth the bother of filling in the form in the hope of getting one in one's own constituency."

Or, from another soldier, asked what he thought was the least encouraging sign for the post-war world as he hoped it would be:

"The least encouraging thing for the post-war world is the reverse of the coin whose obverse is co-operation and discussion. I mean, of course, the cynicism with regard to what will happen after the war which prevails, particularly in the services, and the feeling that the vote is little good. In the Army men are still willing to talk about the way they would like the country run after the war, but nearly always end the discussion by saying: 'What's the use, anyway? It'll be the same old story this time. The old gang will still hold the reins and tell us just where we get off, and that'll mean the dole for most of us, I shouldn't be surprised.'"

Apathy and disinterest are the easy explanations. But from the mass of evidence at our disposal about the development of public feeling and attitude over the war years, we can say with certainty that the real explanation goes deeper. In the political sphere, as in other spheres, people are losing faith in the goodwill and potentialities of authorities. "Whatever you do you get the same thing." It does not mean that they are apathetic in their minds, that they don't *care* what happens. Probably more people care more to-day than ever before. But they feel they're out of the picture, that all the great hierarchies of organisation by which lives are increasingly ordered aren't really *concerned* with them and their wants and needs. Leadership in general is becoming suspect, and with it the elaborate established machinery which leadership controls. This applies to the Churches as it does to the political parties. Goodwill and hope centre increasingly on the individual, the person and not the programme, the actions and not the ideals. It is not chiefly that people are losing faith in ideals and objectives, but that they are losing hope of the capacity and desire of those in prominent positions to help realise those desires. Apathy is the apathy of frustration more than of thoughtlessness.

The return of Labour in the 1945 election was one of several last efforts to make "a better world." Much more than party or country depends on the next year or two of Labour government. It can underline, accelerate, or possibly transfigure, the disillusion of so many Britons.

The scepticism of ordinary people about those in positions of authority reflects back as a scepticism of those in authority about ordinary people. It is an interaction dangerous to democracy. For the longer ordinary people continue sceptical, the more likely is it that scepticism will develop into apathy. And they are likely to become more uncritically susceptible to the appeals of a new revelation which offers fulfilment of their needs through a programme mystical or apocalyptic, synthetic or symbolic, anything new and unencumbered with the old suspicions.

World War II ends with large numbers of young people expecting World War III in their middle age or before. The habit of seeing the future as a reflexion of the past is becoming ingrained in many minds, and makes for the easy frustrated cynicism of "I told you so" when events run true to precedent. In this report we have dealt chiefly with religion and ethics—not very deeply, but at the level of casual conversation which is the level of social intercourse. We find animosities centring on the institution—the Church; a negative goodwill towards the individual priest; a more positive goodwill towards those who have really got this thing, faith; and towards religion itself a broad vague feeling that it is a good thing, that forms and dogma and ritual don't matter much but that it's good to have something to believe in. The pattern we have outlined for religion repeats itself in the area of politics. As the swing away from institutionalised religion has been inaccurately characterised as a swing *towards* something definite, such as atheism, secularism, rationalism—so the current swing away from established political parties has been inadequately characterised as a swing *towards* a particular party, or, more vaguely, to the left. But all the evidence suggests that these undoubted changes of attitude are not chiefly directed toward anything new. The swing away is *not* yet a swing towards anything definite or formulated. At all sorts of levels people have decided what *not* to believe or believe in; they have yet to pick on the alternative. Take five personal accounts, written shortly before the end of the European war, of the way in which people feel their outlook has changed over the past six years. First, an assistant cashier in the early thirties:

"The main effect the war is having on my mind and general outlook on life is to make me rather more cynical than ever as to the aftermath of it all. Two years ago I began to believe that a change of heart might after all be possible among the leaders of the world, but the events of the past year have shaken that opinion badly. Promises are made as glibly as ever and broken as rapidly. People are looking for the loopholes to evade their obligations in this matter and in that. . . ."

Second, a fifty-two-year-old housewife:

"The war is having a deep effect on my mind and of those I meet—a different effect from the last war when I was twenty-one to twenty-five. Then I felt sure we had done right to fight and that a new world would arise. Now I am sceptical and often bitter. When this war *did* come I felt we couldn't escape it by being pacifists, though I'd have done *anything* to prevent it. I have grown more and more disillusioned, and the good qualities brought out by war (courage, endurance, etc.) are so feeble compared with the bad qualities (greed and cruelty) that sometimes I despair of human nature. I cling desperately to anything *good* I find, hoping that however small it is, it will leaven the whole in time. . . ."

Third, a Civil Servant:

"Rather cynical about the future. All this uncertainty of ever getting a decent job—thought of so many restrictions for years to come—probably so little money. In fact, the main effect is a rather cynical attitude towards my own future, the country's future, the world's future."

Fourth, a middle-aged jeweller:

"Utterly fed up with every aspect of the war, and have few ambitions or aims in life now. I think this mood is rather common among persons of the middle classes (and of middle age). What is there to look forward to in the next twenty years?"

Finally, a woman ex-member of the Salvation Army:

"The one predominating effect war has had is this—I scoff at organised religion. Once a uniformed member of the

Salvation Army—but now I see how wrong they are! Uniform still appeals to me very much—but only saints should wear uniforms. Religion is what we make it—either a club or a deep personal experience. War has pointed this out to me because war has dragged me out of it all. Where I used to be in it all day, now I've had to stand aside and so get a new view. In future, I'm a free-thinker, interested in everyone's religion, but belonging to none in particular. War has also given me a new self-confidence and a hard-boiled outlook on anything and everything. I've come to the conclusion that everyone is extremely selfish and cruel, and even when peace does come they'd celebrate it on Monday and cut each other throats on Tues. . . ."

These are selected examples, of course, and a discussion of all the changes which people mentioned would take us outside the limits of the present enquiry. But it is abundantly clear, from numerous studies made during the past years, that this sort of basically negative, protective scepticism has increased and shows no present sign of diminishing. It is a scepticism which is inherently susceptible to anything new and un-implicated in the past, because it is not a positive questioning of anything and everything, but a selective rejection of things which seem to conform to the suspect familiar pattern. The decline of religious faith, documented here, means that people are looking more and more for their hope and aim and fulfilment in earthly things; and earthly programmes, *pro tem.*, seem inadequate. We have concentrated, perhaps overmuch, on a particular group of symptoms, and said little about the hopes which are still very much alive and the energies which have not become neutralised in the drift away from past stabilities. There is, to-day, an enormous fund of dammed-up energy which may be released by an unexpectedly small stimulus. People are looking for something on which to focus the hopes they are holding in check. With the release of the compulsory communal frustrations of war we may expect private frustrations to become more acute and urgent.

Symptoms of the search for something to believe in, unless intelligently and intelligibly canalised from above, may be expected to appear soon. If our interpretation is correct, the alternative to a revival of faith in the near future is a real apathy, of the sort liable to let anything by on the grounds of "I told you so." But the very urgency of the need is itself a danger. People to-day are in a state of mind which may make them over-susceptible to a new panacea. The immediate future hangs very much on the capacity of established leadership and established hierarchies to reinstate themselves in public esteem. If they fail, the new faith which arises as an alternative to apathy will depend very much on what offers. Because the old ideas fail to satisfy, there is no good reason to suppose that people will look more closely at new ones before accepting them. Rather the reverse. The starving spirit is not hypercritical of new food.

SUMMARY OF CONCLUSIONS

In their report, *Towards the Conversion of England*, the Commission on Evangelism remark on the results of previous Mass-Observation surveys[1] of the attitude of ordinary men and women towards religion:

> "It is open to question which is the more alarming feature, the failure of the Church to attract, or its failure to repel."

The present survey documents this superficial attitude of benevolent neutrality, and seeks to describe its basis, implications, and its relation to other current negativisms. The investigation was mainly carried out in one London suburb, which we call Metrop,[2] but much data already on file from other areas and using various techniques was also consulted.

Not more than one person in ten in Metrop is at all closely associated with any of the churches, and about two-thirds never, or practically never, go to Church. The majority, however—four out of five women and two out of three men—give at least verbal assent to the possibility of there being a God, and most of the rest express doubt rather than disbelief. Uncompromising disbelievers in a Deity amount to about one in twenty.

Irrespective of their own religious beliefs, the majority of people in Metrop consider that religion should be taught in schools. Even among those who openly doubt the existence of God, the majority hold this view. Throughout the survey an attitude of "goodwill" towards the *idea* of religion and religious faith is apparent, frequently in conjunction with a hostile attitude towards the Church, and a personal religious faith of an exceedingly vague and unorthodox kind. Less than a

[1] Reported in *Christian News etter*, Supplement 172, February 10th, 1943.
[2] The identity of the suburb is no secret, but it is kept anonymous here because several of its parsons, youth leaders, etc., are quoted in the report, and would be readily identifiable if its whereabouts were specified.

third of Church of England churchgoers, for instance, give definite verbal assent to three basic affirmations of the Apostles' Creed. Over 40 per cent. of them express doubt about the possibility of an afterlife.

The nature of this "goodwill" towards religion is indicated in the attitude of people with no religious beliefs themselves, who favour religious instruction to "give the children an idea of what's right and wrong," "to make them civilised," etc. They still feel that some of the ethical principles of Christianity are right, and they know of no other sanction for them, or means of inculcating them, than the religious one.

To very many religion has come to mean little more than being kind and neighbourly, doing good when opportunity arises. Belief in the Golden Rule, common factor of numerous religious and ethical systems, persists, but without the sanction of faith, or any other sanction than habit and vague memories of childhood teaching.

Throughout this survey we find little difference between the outlook of more and less educated people. The main differences are ones of sex and age. Women in all respects show greater interest in religion than men, more personal faith, and in general a greater respect for religion, whether or not they are themselves "religious." Anti-religious sentiments, as opposed to anti-Church sentiments, come predominantly from men. Both in regard to formal observances and general attitude, the younger generation show a much more critical outlook, and *much less interest*. Two young people (under forty) express doubt about the existence of God for every older person who does so. It is mostly the younger generation who dismiss religion with apparent disinterest, while the old, whatever their own beliefs or lack of beliefs, usually show respect for it.

Broadly speaking, criticism of religion comes most from those groups who are least interested, least informed.

Criticism and disillusion centres chiefly on *organised* religion, on the Churches and their dignataries, on the ostentatious *practice* of religion, rather than on religion itself.

This scepticism about organised religion, about the established hierarchy and leadership, runs parallel with other growing scepticisms. Thus, while ordinary people to-day have increasingly positive ideas about politics and political programmes, their generalised attitude towards politicians and political parties is increasingly one of disillusion and cynicism.

A distrust of established leadership pervades people's minds to-day. While conscious recognition and spontaneous discussion of the problems of the future have perhaps never been so widespread and urgent as they are now; while more people than ever before are aware of what they feel *should* be done; and while these ideas often correspond closely with the expressed ideals of party programme and Christian ethic—still a great gulf of distrust stretches between leaders and people, mass organisation, and disorientated mass.

The potential scope for imaginative, dynamic leadership to-day is immense. Current loss of faith (in religion, in politics, in progress, in science, and so on) is very largely a loss of faith in the unwieldy, centralised, remote *organisation*, which increasingly monopolises the potential realisation of ideals, and which seems so distant and uncontrollable to ordinary people.

These ordinary people are looking for something to believe in. As the need becomes more urgent, so their capacity for discrimination is likely to diminish. If any one overriding conclusion arises from the present report it is this: Established leadership is becoming increasingly remote from ordinary people. If it does not re-establish contact soon, unattached loyalties and desires may well find a focus in some new leadership, uncritically accepted because it succeeds in establishing direct contact with immediate, long-felt human needs. The decline in religious faith is but one symptom of an all-round decline of faith in the future, accelerated by war, accentuated by the inevitable anxieties of peace. The need for faith, whether religious or secular, is shown to be acute, though only partially articulate as yet.

Whether pre-existing faiths re-establish themselves or new faiths arise, is a matter which seems likely to settle itself within the next few years—for people cannot carry on for long in the profoundly negative frame of mind which characterises the short-term outlook of so many to-day.

In the political sphere, the election of a Labour Government in 1945—a change forecast and analysed by Mass-Observation eighteen months before the event[1]—represents for many a last hope within the existing range of political parties and programmes. Much more than immediate considerations of party and country depend on the success or failure of the Labour Party in re-establishing a dynamic relationship with the people of Britain in the next two or three years.

And, if our analysis is correct, the search for a basic faith sanctioning accepted standards of conduct makes the immediate future actions of the established Church of equally vital importance to future stabilities. The persistence of the Christian ethic to-day rests on extremely flimsy foundations. Majority goodwill remains in the current attitude of benevolent neutrality. But, at present, goodwill persists largely for want of alternative. If alternative offers it may be seized on hungrily, uncritically and irrevocably. "The Conversion of England," if it is to be accomplished by the Established Church, will have to be accomplished soon.

[1] "Who'll Win," by Tom Harrisson, *Political Quarterly*, January 1944.